# Grow You, Grow Your Profits

(Discover What's Inhibiting Business Earnings)

Richard F. Corrigan

Copyright © 2017 Richard F. Corrigan

All rights reserved.

ISBN: 1544868480
ISBN-13: 9781544868486

# DEDICATION

This book is dedicated to the glory of God.

Matthew 19:26 (NIV)
"Jesus looked at them and said, 'With man this is impossible, but with God all things are possible'."

## CONTENTS

|  |  |  |
|---|---|---|
|  | Acknowledgments | I |
| 1 | How Is Your Morale? | 1 |
| 2 | Morale Building | 9 |
| 3 | More on Morale Building | 18 |
| 4 | Sales with No Sales Staff | 27 |
| 5 | Listening to Your Competition | 35 |
| 6 | When Should You Ask for Help? | 44 |
| 7 | You Can Lead A Horse to What? | 52 |
| 8 | Focus Focus Who's Got the Focus? | 59 |
| 9 | But I Can't Follow the Plan! | 66 |
| 10 | An Entrepreneurial Day | 74 |

| 11 | **Does the Hat Fit?** | 83 |
| 12 | **A Balancing Act** | 91 |
| 13 | **Looking for Love in All the Wrong Places** | 98 |
| 14 | **A Company Analysis—Part One** | 106 |
| 15 | **A Company Analysis—Part Two** | 114 |
| 16 | **An Exercise: The Cause or the Symptoms** | 122 |
| 17 | **Conclusion** | 129 |

## ACKNOWLEDGMENTS

Grow You, Grow Your Profits was a quarter of a century in the making, made real by the grace of God. This nonfiction book was also made possible by the patience of my spouse, Diana, who always let me verbalize my concerns as I waded through the quagmire of entrepreneurial swamps threatening to sink even the most well-known businesses.

Additional thanks go to all those business owners who realized that they needed assistance in making their companies more profitable and were willing to change themselves to help their bottom line.

# Chapter 1

# How Is Your Morale?

Whether you are at the threshold of starting a business or you're searching for a missing piece of the business-success puzzle, one thing is for sure: at various times there will be enormous hurdles strewn across your path on your way to becoming successful and profitable. The key is to be intellectually, mentally, and emotionally ready when those challenges appear.

To prepare for managing your business successfully, you need to do two things:

1. learn about operating a business
2. learn about yourself

Simple right? But maybe not. For as intent and driven you may be to operate a thriving business, your viewpoint (or personal prejudice—your ego) will color your company decisions, possibly causing you to make unprofitable choices. Having a true understanding of your strengths and weaknesses is paramount to operating a profitable business.

I am sure you have read and heard of the numerous causes of diminishing profitability. Causes like: he was not cut out to run a company, or the economy turned upside down, or a large competitor came into the area and undersold his product line.

The problem with these causes however, is that they would have only become evident to you if your viewpoint had been untainted by prejudice. If your perspective is biased, problems will sneak up on you, hidden, masked—right before your eyes—and you will not see them.

It's like watching someone's hair turn gray. You see him day in and day out and all of a sudden you notice, "Boy, is Larry graying." Actually, Larry had been graying for three years, but you were not sensitive enough to notice. Seeing him everyday, desensitized you to the reality of the situation.

In an effort to learn from someone else's mistakes, we are going to follow Larry Ashley for a few chapters and observe how he operates his business.

\*\*\*

### *The Saga of Larry Ashley*

Larry began his business with little capital and a great amount of enthusiasm and conviction, but he does not have the passion and the drive anymore. Somewhere along the line, he lost them both. However, it did not happen quickly. It was slow, very slow. He did not even notice until it was blatantly obvious.

### *Growth from creativity:*

Business growth stems from creativity—creativity of product, marketing, advertising, production, manufacturing, managing, and more.

Creativity is the egg from which the entrepreneur hatches his business. And, similar to all fledglings, the fastest growth occurs in the months or years just after birth. But, that is also when the greatest amount of training must take place to insure the continued life of the fledgling. That's when the groundwork must be laid—never to be forgotten.

*Larry needed to stay creative. He needed to stay focused on what caused his company to grow.*

Some questions we need to ask are:

1. When did his creativity begin to wane?
2. Why did he lose his creativity?
3. When did he lose it?
4. Could he have made a comeback?
5. Can he come back now?
6. Why couldn't he have seen the warning signs?

There are some things that Larry could have done to help prevent his undoing and other adjustments he could have made to correct the things that went awry.

## *The Signals:*

One of the signals that would indicate your business could be heading in the wrong direction—and that your enthusiasm could be waning—is your company's "community" morale. If morale is not up to par, there has to be a reason. Usually, an obvious manifestation of low morale shows up in the attitudes of some of the key employees.

So, first we need to know:

1. What could they be thinking?
2. What are the thoughts in an employee's mind that could affect his or her morale?

Let's look at a partial list of possible beliefs in an employee's brain:

1) This is a great place to work:
    a) I feel important.
    b) I'm appreciated.
    c) My opinion matters.
    d) My suggestions are used.
    e) I'm complimented.
    f) I'm rewarded.

2) This is the worst place to work:
    a) Conditions stink:
        1) The place is dirty.
        2) It's too cold, too hot.
        3) The equipment is falling apart.
    b) The boss is a jerk
    c) The pay is lousy.

d) No benefits.
   e) The hours stink.
   f) The employees stink.

3) I love my job but:
   a) Low pay.
   b) Boss is a jerk.
   c) People are jerks.

All the negative thoughts inside an employee's mind are basically the result of the employee's physical and emotional surroundings and spell out to the employee one root reason circumstances are the way they are — "The boss doesn't care." And conversely, all the positive thoughts translate into, "The boss cares."

Signs of low morale are sometimes so subtle you might not see them:

1. Employees are spending more time on break.
2. They come back from lunch later than usual.
3. Start later at the beginning of the day.
4. Leave earlier at the end of the day.
5. They huddle more and more and do not have open conversations when the boss is near.
6. They seem to be cooperative enough, but the volunteering has stopped, and "working with a smile" has gone by the wayside.

We contracted with a company where, when we first walked into the office—an office that housed ten people—there was not a sound coming from anyone. As we stayed day after day, sometimes hours would pass without a single communication among the workers.

It was like working in a morgue. There were no smiles, jokes, or stories, and certainly no camaraderie. They showed up, did their jobs, and left when it was time. They were on the time clock, but they took lots of time off: they called in sick, had emergencies, were late because of the dog, or family problems, etc.

Each day it was something new, but the end result was the same—they were spending less time at work. They were willing to take home less money because they hated where they worked.

Their morale was low, but the boss didn't understand it that way. He just thought he employed people who were not dedicated. (Some of these people had been with the company for thirty years and had seen three owners come and go. If that's not dedication...) Consequently, he thought less and less of them, as did they of him.

So, why did he think less and less of his employees? I'm sure you've heard the phrase, *"The art of being yourself at your best is the art of unfolding your personality into the person you want to be. . . . Be gentle with yourself, learn to love yourself, to forgive yourself, for only as we have the right attitude toward ourselves can we have the right attitude toward others."* Wilfred Peterson—modern-day poet.

Well, that was one of Larry Ashley's problems.

Larry grew up in a situation where, according to his parents, he could never do anything right. "That was stupid, Larry. Don't you think first, Larry? Do it over, Larry; it's wrong. You stay until your work is done.

You're lazy, Larry."

"But, Dad, you leave. You arrive late. You take a break."

"I'm the boss. I can do what I want. You can't."

These phrases continually echo inside Larry's head. So when he became the boss, he only continued thinking and doing what he had learned as a child. His viewpoint was biased.

**WTGB** (Words to Grow By)—The boss should play by the same rules as the employees.

**WTGB**—Keeping your personal morale high will make you sensitive to your employees' morale.

So Larry didn't notice the low morale of his employees because it fit right into his own mental state of mind. He was driving into the sun.

His personal morale was low, so where was there a problem? He viewed the employee problems the same way his parents viewed his immaturity when he was younger: as laziness, being uncommitted, undedicated; deserving low wages, poor working conditions, and never a kind word.

In fact, the only words Larry ever had for any of his employees were criticisms or insults.

Why? Because finding fault with his employees was what he knew how to do. He had been trained since childhood.

**WTGB**—Always find something good to say to an employee. Make sure it revolves around the job or the company, not anything personal.

It was not that Larry's employees were nonperformers, it was that Larry, deep down in his subconscious mind, felt *he* was a nonperformer, and the only way he could go home each day and feel as if he amounted to anything, was to unconsciously and irrepressibly put down his workers.

**WTGB**—Keep a positive motivational book in your office, and when you feel yourself becoming negative, grab it, read a little, let it sink in for a few minutes, and then get back to work with a more positive frame of mind.

So what has Larry created? A low morale situation that, because he has created it, he does not recognize it as the problem it is, but as something else.

**WTGB**—Because you are the boss, all eyes and ears are on you, so you always should be creating a positive morale situation.

# Chapter 2

# Morale Building

Larry Ashley scowled when his secretary announced that his wife was on the phone.

"Larry, what's your gun doing on the nightstand?" Noelle asked as she held the steal weapon in her trembling hand.

"I was just looking at it," Larry said with a dismissive tone.

"Looking at it when? And for what reason?" Noelle asked, her concern bleeding through the telephone line.

"I forgot to put it away," Larry said, side-stepping the questions, his glazed eyes staring out the window at the truck leaving the loading dock still full of its COD-supply load meant for his company.

"Larry, I want you to get some help," Noelle said.

"I'm okay, I can handle it."

"Larry, call David."

Larry mumbled something, said goodbye, and walked out to the warehouse.

***

This day had not progressed well. First, Larry had two disagreements with his staff. And now, his wife thought Larry needed to see someone about his problems.

"They all think they know more than me about this business," Larry said.

Remember the different thoughts in employees' minds? Larry's workers felt he didn't care. Why did they feel this way? For some time now, Larry has only shown concern for himself and the company.

Somehow, Larry has to value his people once more and get them reenergized in growing the business again. They were before—back when *Larry* was all fired up with enthusiasm and drive.

You may know one thing Larry could do: listen to his people.

**WTGB**—Take time to listen to your employees. Do not listen only once a year at their annual review. Schedule informal sessions over coffee, lunch, in the back of the warehouse, on a walk around the block. Stroll through the company with a cup of coffee in your hand. This sends a friendlier message instead of "watch out, here comes the boss."

The other thing Larry could do is get his people involved—involved in a cause that would help him turn his company around.

Some business advisors readily suggest that to raise morale, you need to give your employees an increase in pay. The problem with that scenario is that sometimes in the employee's eyes, the raise may not be significant. And whatever the amount, after a couple of months, "the thrill is gone."

**WTGB**—Don't believe that it is enough to give an employee a job and a salary. Sometimes, involving an employee in a project will light within him a huge fire of enthusiasm.

But what else could be done?

**WTGB**—Involve your employees in brainstorming sessions to help find solutions for the difficulties you are facing with your business.

Old-school management would tell the boss to keep his business problems to himself, but that assumed the boss not only had all the answers but also knew the right questions to ask. The employees may or may not have the answers, but they may have the right questions that, when answered, may help the company.

Let's say that Larry had begun having periodic meetings with his staff early on to draw out their questions and suggestions about the operation of his business.

You have to remember that, since you operate a small business, you probably do not have a board of directors.
In the past, the entrepreneur's unnamed board

included his insurance agent, his banker, his attorney, and his accountant. Today, the quartet is missing the banker because many are now sales reps, and accountants, attorneys, and insurance agents have become too specialized.

But, in this case, Larry's ego got in the way.

Let's stop for a moment and ruminate on the subject of ego. Throughout this exposé, you will notice the suggestion that many business problems stem from a blemish on the owner's ego. The ego is the most vital and, at the same time, most dangerous business tool. At times it can be a wonderful asset, and within moments it can transform itself into the company's largest liability.

It takes a certain amount of ego to step out and become an entrepreneur. You have to believe in yourself. You have to have guts, thick skin, and mettle. And an ego provides much of what is needed.

However, that same ego can prevent you from asking for help, seeing problems, taking advice, reacting to situations, etc. Egos are great in their place. Michael Jordan's ego was his best friend. And the world admired him. Conversely, Hitler's ego almost destroyed the world.

Big businesses are usually guided by a board of directors. Small businesses are not. This is not to say that the presidents of large businesses do not have egos, or that they themselves sometimes do not get in the way of their operation. But a big business usually has a board of directors that keeps the ego of the point person in check.

Think of it this way, how do you act at home with your spouse, alone at night, without the kids around? Then, how do you act around your boss without your spouse around?

We tend to take on certain personality aspects as is appropriate to interface in the most positive manner with whomever we are with at the time. Our ego molds and fashions itself to meet the circumstance and the person in our presence.

Now think about how you act when you are in the company of both your spouse and your boss at the same time. Your ego is altered slightly to accommodate each person. Now, think of having a meeting with a board of directors comprised of fourteen business leaders, how would you act with them?

But alone, in your own domain, on your own turf and being the boss, the power of your ego is sometimes too much to control.

**WTGB**—The better and more secure you feel about yourself in relation to those around you, the more able you are to exercise positive mental control over your ego.

And what causes an out-of-control ego? A poor self-image. The inferior the image, the larger the ego seems to loom over the personality of the individual—thus affecting all perspective. Our ego acts as our personal champion. Our Bodyguard. Our ego protects us from pain by keeping us on the attack and by warding off emotionally debilitating missiles.

Larry felt he could and had to do it all. But although he gave birth to the idea that began his business, he did not have the financial, sales, and management skills to operate his company successfully. But he could have.

If he had taken the time to surround himself with employees who would complement his shortcomings, he would now have a working board in place—an ad-hoc board of directors.

**WTGB**—Surround yourself with employees who know more than you in the specific areas you have shortcomings.

But Larry's employees did not seem committed—they only participated as a result of their need to receive a paycheck at the end of the week. Their engagement in the company was secondary to their need to circumvent any new amount of work that the boss could dump on them.

**WTGB**—Find your leaders—people who manage the employees even though they do not have the titles.

There was one employee in Larry's company who seemed to be more discontented than all the rest. If Larry could have involved that employee in the company, he might have had a handle on the problems he was facing before they became unmanageable.

**WTGB**—Do not read a discontented employee as one who will not and cannot work hard for the company. Maybe he needs a major project to rekindle that fire that was there when he first arrived. Maybe she is a prophet who can foresee things you cannot.

**WTGB**—Call your employees individually into your office and tell them of your desire to grow the company to a new level. Then ask for their ideas about what they think would be needed to reach that level.

Sometimes, it's hard to listen when an employee who earns just two dollars an hour above minimum wage tells you that you are going in the wrong direction—that you are not seeing the rock up ahead in the middle of the road. Larry had trouble listening to his employees.

**WTGB**—Listening to your employees demonstrates your intelligence not your weakness. Not listening, demonstrates your ignorance.

Sometimes your employees can see things that are invisible to you, and they may come up with suggestions that can help you get your business back on track.

**WTGB**—If you listen to their observations, they will perceive that you care about them and the company—and they too will care.

It is an enormous boost to employee morale when the boss listens to what the they have to say. And it is an even bigger boost when he acts on a worker's suggestion. The ultimate high comes when the rest of the company is together, and you let them know that the new procedure was not your idea, but Angie's.

And when you can afford it, buy her and her significant other dinner, or buy them tickets to a movie. It doesn't have to be extravagant. Even a card of thanks will do more than nothing at all.

The employees need to take ownership of the company, figuratively. And they will if you let them become more involved in creating methods and procedures to make the company more profitable.

Additionally, finding out how to make the day more pleasant for your staff, whether it be by sitting them in a more comfortable chair, providing better lighting, or allowing them to move to the other side of the office to better hear the intercom, will do more for them and the company, on a permanent basis, than handing out small raises that are used up within the first week.

\*\*\*

An out-of-state client had an employee who found every way possible to use up the day without accomplishing assigned tasks. She kept getting progressively further behind. She was the most negative employee—silently crying out for acknowledgment. She knew how to help the company, but the boss viewed her as a chronic complainer.

Upon our advisement, she was asked to undertake a major project. It did not bring with it a raise or bonus, because there was not any money to do that, and he did not change her job title. The owner did tell her she was the only person, who could do the job successfully. And that the company, the boss, and the rest of the employees needed her to do it. That was the truth.

After a long weekend of soul-searching, she came into

work on Tuesday morning and agreed to take on the project. When the rest of the workforce saw her attitude change, and the intensity with which she attacked the project, they fell like dominoes and joined in with renewed enthusiasm.

Eventually, they all had equally important projects. Morale turned around. Creativity reigned. And it didn't cost a thing. But, at the end of the year, there was more money for raises and every employee's paycheck grew.

**WTGB**—Do not be afraid to turn responsibilities over to your employees or to take the time to listen to their concerns.

Many of Larry's staff had been with the company for seven years. He reminded us of Ebenezer Scrooge when we asked him to tell us his employees' names. There were only twenty-two of them, and he new almost none of their last names. And some of the ones he thought he did know, he got wrong.

**WTGB**—Know your employees' names, their spouses', their kids', and where they live. Pay attention to the cars they drive, how they dress, and where they go out to eat. The better you know your employees, the better a manager you will be—and the better a manager you are, the more profitable your business will be.

# Chapter 3

# More on Morale Building

Noelle Ashley sat at her desk in the study of their suburban home and pondered her dilemma. Her husband, Larry, was becoming more and more distraught; she found a gun by his bedside last month. She finally decided to call her friend, David Harper.

Hearing the stress in Noelle's voice, David immediately asked what the problem was.

"Has Larry called you?" Noelle asked.

"No. Is he supposed to?" David asked as he reached for a pad of paper.

"He needs help with his business, but he won't ask for it. Last month I told him to call you. David, I'm really concerned. I suspect the company's going under."

"Is there money coming in?"

"Yes, but not enough to cover the daily operating expenses. If only Larry could have seen the signals."

"Maybe he did, but chose to ignore them."

**Signals!**

What are they but subtle prophecies of the future.

When heeded—disaster can be averted.

When ignored—disaster always follows.

Larry's employees' low morale could have warned him. But Larry was not sensitive enough. He was too self-absorbed.

**WTGB**—Focus attention away from yourself—your problems, feelings, and concerns—and look to the needs of your employees.

Months ago, when Larry's staff began to lose hope in their company, they started to drift away. There was no goal to shoot for and no cheerleader to spur them on. Larry's method of motivation was the same as a taskmaster; he cracked the whip and gave his employees one day in seven to rest. If he had to work, so did they. So you might say that at least they got overtime. Not so. Larry staggered their hours so that they had to come to work six days a week, yet only worked 40 hours.

**WTGB**—Praising your employees and communicating your expectations is better than always pointing out what they are doing wrong.

If Larry had continually set new goals for his employees and continued to instill hope and express confidence in their ability to reach those goals, their morale would not have collapsed.

Companies and organizations grow fastest when first beginning. The next spurt of growth is either under new leadership or as a result of the introduction of a new product or service.

Much can be learned from how church congregations grow. Church attendee numbers increase in greater spurts when there is a cause: a new roof, an organ, a new wing, or sponsoring a mission village. If the individual members are idle, they tend to lose their positive morale and begin to drift away, mentally and spiritually—bickering amongst themselves and finding fault with everything; and consequently, volunteering diminishes.

But what kind of goals should Larry have set?

1.  Sales goals are always good to declare, post, and pursue. They have to be attainable (or at least believed to be attainable) and you must communicate them to the whole of your organization, not just to the sales people.

2.  Operational goals are also good: a goal of reaching a certain efficiency in production or customer-service response.

Of course, setting the goals is only just the beginning. There has to be a plan to reach those goals and proportional rewards for doing so. Larry could have begun by having brain-storming sessions to break down the goals into management benchmarks that, once attained, would give each member of his staff a sense of accomplishment and a boost in morale.

Other goals could include: advertising, marketing, distribution, production, and working-space physical configuration.

Larry's employees spent more waking hours at work than they did with their own families or in their own homes. A small thing Larry could have done with very little expense would have been to allow his employees to arrange the office area to suit their individual and group needs. They had been sitting in the same positions in the same chairs with the same desks for years.

Some of them needed a bigger space, some wanted a smaller space. Some wanted to be nearer each other, and others wished to be farther away. Some wanted to decorate their space but were apprehensive. Larry could have given them power over their own areas and let them work out the logistics of the day-to-day workflow.

One of his employees was known for her slowness at accomplishing her tasks at her desk. After nonchalantly observing her for a couple of days, we sadly could only come up with one solution; and that was to offer her early retirement.

But then something strange happened. We noticed that when she answered the phone (she was fourth in line to answer it if the other three designated employees were tied up), she picked it up with her left hand and then switched it to her right hand so she could write, stretching the phone cord across the desk in front of her and in her way.

That's when we noticed that her entire work area was

set up for a right-handed person and she was left-handed! She had never felt she had the right to change it because it was that way (seven years ago) when she took the job. We immediately suggested, with the Larry's blessing, that she change her work area around to suit her.

Her efficiency shot through the roof. It wasn't just because she now had a left-handed work area, that was part of it, but the fact that the boss cared enough to allow her to rearrange her world made the difference.

Another aspect that helps build morale is the general cleanliness of the work environment. If the floors, desks, file cabinets, break-room, and bathrooms are dirty; the employees' perception is that the boss doesn't care if they live like animals.

**WTGB**—Keep your work area and the area your employees work in clean and neat. Setting the example goes further than the old, "Don't do as I do, do as I say."

Larry had not paid for any cleaning services for months, and he made no contingency plan except to ask the warehouse workers to clean up and take out the trash when he thought of it. The employees began to wear more "work-in-the-yard clothes" with the explanation, "Why should we wear our good clothes and have them ruined?"

If Larry could not afford to pay for a cleaning service, he should have set aside a Saturday morning to clean his company himself. That's what many entrepreneurs have to do when they begin. Why not when the dollars get tight? In fact, Noelle would have gladly helped if Larry had only asked.

If Larry loses, Noelle loses, too.

Larry was not fighting any longer. He was not fighting to keep his company or his employees. He had developed a passive rather than active approach to his situation.

**WTGB**—Spend some of your management time as a cheerleader and a facilitator.

**WTGB**—If and when you encounter a problem, attack it. If left unattended, it will multiply like rats or cockroaches and consume everything that is vital to your business.

What if Larry had recognized he had a problem? What if he had sought some professional help? What if he had begun to deal with the echoes in his head?

Instead, he gave up on creativity and relied on policing.

A business seems to operate within three stages, fluctuating between each stage throughout its life.

1. **Creative Stage:** The first stage is the creative stage. This is where the largest business growth occurs.

2. **Management Stage:** Many times however, an entrepreneur will forget what he did to arrive at a business's current level of growth and begins to devote all of his time to managing the day to day operations, and the people within his empire. This second stage is the

management stage. When the entrepreneur begins to manage, business—most times—begins to diminish.

3. **Policing Stage:** As business falls off and funds tighten, the entrepreneur slips into the policing stage. The policing stage is where he second-guesses everything and micro-manages. Unless he returns to the creative stage, he will soon be out of business.

Larry felt he was beyond learning anything new. He felt that if he admitted he did not know something, his employees would think less of him. They would think him stupid.

And what did the employees really think of him? They felt sorry for him. They thought he was a decent person who did not know the first thing about managing people or a business. They thought he really did not care about them or the business. (They had not received a raise in over two years.) They had no benefits—Larry took them away when money got tight. But Larry drove a new car, went on extravagant vacations, and always talked about the new toy he had just purchased.

**WTGB**—Continually give yourself a reality check. Be as objective as possible. Are you flaunting your personal life?

**WTGB**—Owning your own business and working hard entitles you to some rewards, just keep your rewards to yourself. Telling your employees of your latest purchase or vacation, will only foster ill feelings.

Sometimes it is difficult to recognize when you have a

problem. And when you do recognize it, sometimes it's difficult to admit it. But that, as always, is the first step. It is not easy. It is altering an ego that has worked so hard to protect you. And your ego is the size it is, based on your self-image.

**WTGB**—If you feel bad about yourself, do something about it. Fill your mind with positive thoughts. Do something productive. Volunteer for something.

The fact that you need to learn more, means just that—not that you're stupid. You would be stupid if, after you concluded that you needed to learn more, you didn't. Or refused to. The fact that you never received a college education does not make you inferior to all those who have. Neither should the fact that you are divorced make you feel less of a person than those who are not or who have never married. The fact that you would still be working in the line at the factory if it were not for daddy buying you the business, should be driven completely out of your head.

Altering and controlling your ego is one of the most difficult tasks you will ever encounter, but the end result will bring you true enlightenment and a freedom you will cherish for the rest of your life.

You will develop more sensitivity, kindness, and better people skills. Controlling your ego will allow you to feel good about surrounding yourself with people who know more than you. Turning responsibilities over to your employees will be effortless. Standing aside and letting them run with the ball will bring you a feeling of accomplishment. And you will actually enjoy saying, "I don't know, teach me."

***

It was five o'clock. Larry sighed and finally got around to unfolding the note his wife gave him when he had left for work that morning. He read it and crumpled it with contempt, throwing it into the trash can as he slapped the light switch and walked out the door. "Thank God this day is over," he muttered.

The silence in his empty office was negated by the crumpled note straining to unfold.

**WTGB**—If someone has taken the time to write you a note, keep it for a while and reread it a couple of times. You may learn something.

# Chapter 4

## Sales With No Sales Staff

It was 3:45 PM, Christmas Eve. The snow was lightly falling on the pot-holed, asphalt parking lot outside Ashley Supply Company. ASC's only sales representative walked into Larry's office. The conversation went like this:

"I'm here to get my October's commission check you promised me," Eddy Lang said with noticeable contempt.

"I don't have it," Larry said, standing to meet Eddy's glare straight on.

"What do you mean you don't have it?" Eddy asked, his voice increasing in volume. The employees in the outer office already knew why Eddy was in the boss's office; he told them he was going to ask Larry for his money. He also told them what he was going to do if Larry didn't give it to him.

Larry walked over and closed the office door. "I mean I don't have it," he said, fixing a glare. "The bank wanted its money, and the suppliers wanted theirs; and when I got through paying everyone's salary, the money was gone."

"What happened to the $20,000 I brought in last week?" Eddy asked, knowing full well what had happened. Marsha in finance told him Larry had to cover his personal bank note for the boat he keeps at his camp up on Lake Masserette.

Eddy made a fist and said, "I want it now, Larry. I charged all my Christmas presents, and when the bills come January 15$^{th}$, I need that money to cover them."

"Maybe I'll have it by then," Larry said.

Eddy knew the money would not be there. That's why for the last three months, his sales had progressively dwindled—he was looking for another job. Eddy turned without saying a word and walked out the door.

\*\*\*

It was now January 12$^{th}$. Larry, with a piece of paper dangling from his hand, was sitting in his office staring out the window. Eddy just had him legally served for back pay, commission, and expenses. All Larry could think about was how ungrateful Eddy was.

Larry paid him for what he did. If it hadn't been for Larry, Eddy wouldn't have had any products to sell to his customers. And at a time when sales were down, how could he jump ship like this? "If anyone calls for a reference, I won't give one," Larry muttered.

\*\*\*

Could this have been foreseen? You bet. The company's sales had been falling all year as a result of

Ashley Supply losing its other two sales representatives. Larry fired one in March, and another in June—both for low production. They claimed prices were not competitive, and the product manufactured by Ashley Supply was behind the times. They were correct, but Larry wouldn't listen.

**WTGB**—Listen to your sales people. Weigh what they say. Do not overreact, but listen.

We will deal with Larry's ego problem later, but what can you do if you do not have or cannot afford a sales representative—if you are the only contact with the outside world? Larry found himself in this predicament at the beginning of a new year.

### *Telling Your Story*

Everyone has a natural sales force just waiting to be tapped. Everyday we carry on conversations with those we meet, unless we choose not to talk to anyone. If you are not talking to anyone, you have a different problem. In any case, think about the pattern of your conversations: you tell stories, get reactions, listen to others tell stories, give reactions, describe problems, ask for solutions, listen to the answers, listen to problems, give advice.

Why can't part of your story be about the product or service you offer? Something like this: You meet a friend on the street on your way to lunch, someone you have not seen in quite a while. We will call your friend Dominique.

1.  You: "Hi Dominique, how are you? It's been quite a while."

2.  Dominique: "I'm fine, what's new?"

3.  You: After a certain amount of personal sharing about each of your families or places you have been, you say, "I'm working on a new project, providing fundraising sources for profit and nonprofit organizations. All I need are three more clients and I'll be set."

4.  Dominique: "What do you do? How do you do it?"

5.  You: "I meet with members of businesses and organizations. I learn what their problems are, how much money they need, and when they need it. Then I provide fundraising solutions."

6.  Dominique: "Like, what kind of solutions?"

7.  You tell your story. How do you provide solutions? What kind of product/service do you sell?

8.  Then you say, "All I need are three more customers, or clients, or sales. I need help. Do you know of anyone <u>who might know of anyone</u> whose brain I could pick for suggestions? I need some guidance and advice."

9.  Dominique: "I may know of someone."

10. In the conversation, you are telling a little of what you do for a living, expressing a goal or need, and asking for help. Additionally, you did not ask Dominique for a direct referral but for an indirect one. *Do you know of anyone <u>who might know of anyone</u> whose brain I could pick for suggestions?*

11. And each time you see your friend, Dominique, she will always ask how things are going. Make sure you tell her your story, state your goal, and ask for help. Tell her you are still looking for some contacts and advice. People love to help.

**WTGB**—Sharing your goals and your needs enlists people as additional eyes and ears. *"Ask, and it shall be given you; seek, and ye shall find; knock, and it shall be opened unto you."* Matt. 7: 7 (Sermon on the Mount—Jesus Christ)

## Listening To Your Sales People

If you own a small company, it is in your best interest to set aside time to noodle with your sales staff and listen, really listen to what they are saying your customers' needs are. Your sales people are the only representatives of your company who are out there with the competition and can see first hand what the competition is offering.

**WTGB**—Stay in touch daily, or at least weekly, with your sales force. They are like scouts in the wilderness.

If you are offering a product and your sales people are beginning to rave about the capabilities of the competitor's product, you should listen. It would be a good idea to invest some time in research and development to make your products better.

\*\*\*

We had occasion to become involved with a manufacturing company that had original patents on three products. A review of the sales figures for the last five years, revealed a very obvious downward trend. The owner blamed it on the economy. The sales representatives said the company offered an inferior product compared to what the competition was offering. Further investigation revealed that there had been no product research and development in the last six years, and thus no resulting product improvements for the past ten years.

**WTGB**—As often as you assess yourself, assess your product. Test, test, test.

Clearly, if your product has not been improved in the last ten years, either it was far superior to anything anyone could reduplicate in that timeframe; which in this day and age is highly unlikely, or you didn't make it part of your plan to improve your product to insure your company's growth. The salespeople are your point persons. They can perform competition surveys. You need this information on an ongoing basis.

**WTGB**—Structure a report that your sales staff must complete on a regular basis which addresses how your product is fairing against the competition.

The sales people may also come back to the office with your competition's prices. They may show you that your product is overpriced. There is a danger in this however. Sometimes, sales people who do not believe in the product they are trying to sell or lack product knowledge or sales ability, will use price as the reason for their inability to attain a larger sales volume.

Also, make sure you are comparing apples to apples. Maybe your product should be priced higher based on a point for point comparison of the benefits your product offers the customer over the competition's. In any case, your competitor's prices are important to you if only because they are important to your customers.

But why wouldn't Larry listen to his sales people?

Again, we have to look at Larry's mindset, his viewpoint:

1.   **First off**: Larry was the one running the company. He felt he didn't have to listen to anyone; they had to listen to him.

2.   **Second**: he is the one who sets the sales goals. The only problem with this is that Larry never set the goals. It was just, "Go out and get the business"—that way, the sales people would always fall short of what Larry expected of them. He could not be placed in a position to praise them. They would not respect him. He was never praised by his father.

3.   **Third**: Larry had to be the best sales person. So, in order to maintain that position, he had to always demand more, claiming that if it weren't for his continual prodding and pushing, the company would have no sales at all.

**WTGB**—You are the number one representative of your company. However, wouldn't it be great if all your sales people outperformed you?

Of course, Larry never went out on sales calls. But he claimed all in-house sales as if he generated them. There was no way to beat Larry. He controlled what became an in-house account.

**WTGB**—Find a way for your sales people to share in the profits of in-house accounts.

Larry never listened to the problems his sales people had. "If you can't solve the problem, then maybe you shouldn't be a salesman," Larry would say. The fact is, he didn't know how to solve the problem, but he couldn't allow his people to know that.

But couldn't Larry have taken a sales course or at least bought a book?

"I don't have to do that, I'm the boss," the echo in his head reminded him.

Although his father died fifteen years ago, Larry was still trying to show his dad how successful he was. The shadow of the "tyrannical boss" loomed over Larry's head, and his ego caused him to aspire to that image.

**WTGB**—You are in charge. Not your relatives. Not your ego. So, be in charge.

**WTGB**—Realize you are not perfect. Realize that you will make mistakes. Realize you have more to learn. Learn more, and believe in yourself.

## Chapter 5

## Listening to Your Competition

Larry Ashley finally called his wife's friend, David Harper, an attorney.

David told Larry that he wasn't an expert in general business management. He said he didn't feel comfortable with giving him any specific advice except to suggest that he create a board of directors to help him through this.

Larry shivered in his cold office. "I can't afford to pay a board of directors," Larry said. "Besides, what would someone else know about my business?"

"Look Larry," David said, "based on what Noelle has told me, you're not ready to listen anyway." David figured he had nothing to lose by being honest.

"I listen when the advice makes sense," Larry said, with a certain amount of defiance.

"Larry, let me give it to you straight, unless you're ready to listen—"

"I told you I do listen," Larry said, raising his voice, cutting David off and standing up behind his desk.

"I wasn't finished," David said, becoming slightly irritated with Larry's demeanor. "I was saying, unless you're ready to listen and not second-guess good advice, you'll just continue in the same direction. How do you think you got into this situation?"

Larry quickly said, "The economy, lazy salesmen, employees who just do enough to get by. No one gives a damn, anymore."

"Larry, you got where you are by not listening. All your decisions caused the circumstance you're in now. Don't you see that?"

Larry began raising his voice again. "All I know is that this is my company, and I'm the one who makes the decisions, and I don't need anyone else's input."

"Larry, you need the advice of other business people who have experienced similar situations. You need to listen to them. You need to do what they did."

"I just need to borrow more money. I'm going to the bank this afternoon, so don't worry yourself. Thanks anyway," Larry said and hung up.

David sat there for a moment staring at the silent receiver in his hand. With controlled frustration, he cradled it onto the carriage.

***

Larry Ashley will not listen. But what are some of the things he should be researching?

For one thing, the competition.

I know you are busy. But you cannot ever be too occupied to know what your competition is doing. Whether you are selling a product or a service, you need to know two basic things: What your company stands for, and what the competition stands for and is doing.

With today's technology, specifically the Internet, there is no reason you cannot find out right from your office or your home computer what your competition is doing.

By making sure you completely understand your competition, you can find loopholes in their product or service offerings that can help you move ahead.

The key is to find out about your competition without them knowing it, and without spending huge chunks of money.

The following are some tips on how to casually, inexpensively, effectively, and unpretentiously find out about your competition:

1) Initiate a customer survey. Make up a form with maybe 5 to 10 questions. Questions like:
    a. Do you like the packaging of the product?
    b. Does the price seem competitive? (Too high? Too low?)
    c. Does the product do what you thought it would?
    d. Do you enjoy dealing with our company?
    e. Do you enjoy dealing with our sales people?
    f. Are there any product improvements you would recommend?
    g. Is the customer service department responsive to your needs?
    h. Are you dealt with in a timely fashion?

i. Is there a clear demonstration of product knowledge by the sales staff?
j. Is there a clear demonstration of product knowledge by the service staff?
k. How did you hear about the company?
l. How did you hear about the Product/Service?
m. What additional products/services should the company offer?
n. What hours should the store be open?
o. How often do you buy?

You can have your sales people ask these questions as they call on their customers, or you can send out a mailer offering discount incentives when the questionnaire is returned. During the survey, information about your competitors will come to light. You can ask each customer who comes into your place of business to fill out a questionnaire while they are waiting for the product or service.

It's always good to provide in bold print at the top of the survey the time it takes to fill out the questionnaire so that your customers know that it will take only 90 seconds to complete the survey.

A customer survey does two things:
- provides you with what your customers feel is important to them
- lets them know you value their opinion.

Most likely, both will result in increased business.

2) Make it a practice of ordering your competition's brochures and catalogs. This will enlighten you as to:

a. What kind of quality are the marketing tools of your competition?
   b. Do they say what yours say?
   c. Should yours say something different?
   d. Should yours say the same as the competition?

Clip your competition's ads:
   a. Analyze what they are saying in them.
   b. How they say it.
   c. To whom they seem to be saying it.
   d. What geographic area do they target?
   e. Is this the same as yours?
   f. Why not?
   g. In what media does your competition advertise: Newspapers? Radio? Magazines? Television? Internet?
   h. What do they have on their webpage?

3) Continually price your competition. Grocery store management is so used to the competition doing this to them, they actually are on a first name basis with the employees of the competition who come and do the shopping.

4) From time to time, buy something from the competition. Of course, if you are selling a service, this may be a little difficult, but maybe you can have the next friend who calls you and asks for your service, do you a favor and have that service performed by the competition—and you offer to split the cost. This would not only give you some insight into the competition's quality of product or workmanship but the style of salesmanship, customer service, and price. It is also a perk

for your friend since you are paying for a portion of his expense. It may also be a business write-off for you.

5) Always, always read the newspapers, the trade magazines and the Internet. You are subscribing anyway. Don't just let them sit for weeks—read them when you first get them. Your competition is advertising in there. There is a wealth of business in a newspaper, whether it is a business paper or the daily news—hard copy or on the Internet. They may even lead you to a client or customer. Or they may spark a new approach to selling your product. Or enlighten you to a new, unexplored market. Or maybe give you ideas of how to operate your company more efficiently and more profitably.

6) Try to be present at least once a month at some sort of business meeting that revolves around the product or service you provide. Your competitors will be there, maybe in the form of a salesperson or an owner, and invariably they will be telling people the latest endeavors of their company. If you listen carefully, you may hear: who, what, when, where, and for how much—information you can use. In your community there are probably a number of Chambers of Commerce and numerous other business organizations. You might consider joining a couple of these groups.

7) Attend trade shows as often as you are able. Many are free, and others are reasonably priced. Hundreds, sometimes thousands of business people attend these shows not only to exhibit, but to see who and what is there.

8) Use networking to its ultimate. There are ways to make networking work for you. Information and Tip clubs are a good source. So are meetings at school, church, and the town hall. Also, the gym.

These are by no means all the things you could do to find out about the competition, but if you only did these eight exercises, you would be developing a habit that could keep you just a little ahead of your competition and well on track to operating a profitable business.

Larry Ashley did not have even one competitor's brochure, catalog, or product in his office. He felt he did not have to know about his competition. He thought he knew all that was needed to run a successful company.

**WTGB**—You can learn from your competition—good and bad.

Why did Larry feel he couldn't learn anything from the competition? Remember, Larry wasn't in control of his thought processes. His ego was in control, causing him to make decisions based on his past, his father's prejudices, and the learned defense strategies brought on by his personal boyhood environment. Consequently, he did everything he could to make himself feel better by reacting to situations in a way that would promote his self-confidence. Larry learned a long time ago that seeing what a competitor was doing, placed him in a situation of knowing that maybe he wasn't doing so well. So he chose not to look.

Larry learned that avoidance protected him from immediate pain. He avoided friends, relatives, acquaintances, and business associates. He avoided even his own wife when he felt there would be a situation that would threaten him. And remember, almost everything threatened him.

**WTGB**—Stay in the mix.

Larry did not want to see what the competition was doing because then he knew that he could or should be doing the same thing. He did not want to feel inadequate, stupid, or lazy.

**WTGB**—If you believe you can learn something from someone, you will. If you don't, you won't.

Everything Larry did, every decision he made or did not make, every thought he had was driven by his learned response and learned feelings about himself. His ego was running the company, and doing a poor job of it.

Who or what is running your company?

Uncontrolled egos are not good managers. They tend to have the attitude that the employees are there for the sole purpose of serving the boss. And that the boss is there to be served, not to serve. Uncontrolled egos see only one side of a situation: How can I best be served? What will result in a better profit for me? What will insure my security?

Uncontrolled egos are not wise. If they were, then the ego's answers to the above questions would be: Serve my employees. Pay the employees better. Insure my employees' security. But the ego can only see one side of a situation, and that side is selfishness and greed.

**WTGB**—Think of your organizational chart as an inverted pyramid with your position at the bottom and your lowest paid employee positions spread across the top.

## Chapter 6

## When Should You Ask for Help?

Larry is still not ready to ask for help. So the question arises, "How long should you wait?" How long can you wait? When should you ask? If you discover that there is a problem in your company, is there a magic increment of time you can delay before bringing in outside help or seeking self-help?

Some offered advice, but basically worthless, is from those who say, "Don't wait too long."

When is too long? Has Larry waited too long? Not really. But let's pick a too-late scenario.

If the sheriff is chaining shut your parking lot gates and attaching a lock for which he has the only key, then it's probably too late. Or if the IRS has announced that all you own is being auctioned at 3:00 P.M., it's probably too late. Or if your last employee has packed up his desk and walked out the door, it's definitely too late.

The key to preventing these scenarios is to ask for help before disaster strikes. The difficulty is recognizing the root of the problem, not the end result of the problem.
For example: What is the reason sales have declined?

Well, it could be that the product is no good, or the price is too high, or the economy is on a downward trend. It could be that the sales staff is not performing. Or is it that the owner does not know how to manage a sales force, or price a product properly, or adjust for a sluggish economy?

The owner, no matter how you excuse the problem away, is ultimately responsible for the success or failure of any and all areas of his/her company. So, if sales are down because the owner does not know how to motivate a sales force, he had better do one of two things: get sales smart, or hire someone who is. The fact that she refuses to act on either of these solutions, is a result of an uncontrolled ego problem that is standing in the way of the admission of ignorance.

**WTGB**—Admitting your ignorance is a testimony to your inner strength.

Predicting when a small business will fail is somewhat like predicting an earthquake. Scientists have become more knowledgeable of the warning signs of earthquakes and can come close to predicting the general area and time of a major event, but the exact time and place the earthquake will strike, still eludes them.

So it is, with the exact time of business failure because of all the variables involved in business operation. It's actually easy to predict whether a business will fail or not. Just look at the owner's response to advice. If he takes advice willingly and applies it freely, the chances of business success are pretty good. If he does not, it's only a matter of time before the doors close.

The more uncontrolled the ego, the more you are prevented from admitting an inadequacy, and the more likely business failure is imminent.

But when should you ask for help?

There is no special formula like:

1) @if(E>95%GS,NPx (15%x$n$E/MILA),OK)
2) @if(1< FB—SC),call for help, OK)

(If expenses are greater than 95% of gross sales, then multiply your net profit by a factor of 15% of the number of employees you have, divided by your mother-in-law's age. If the number is less than the age of your first born child minus your charge card's monthly payment, then call for help, otherwise you're OK.)

I wish it were that simple, but it takes a good amount of introspection to reach the point when you discover you need help.

*First of all*, you have to notice that your employees are becoming more discontented with their jobs and their surroundings. They may voice it in a joking fashion or in hostile outbursts during or outside structured meetings.

These outbursts are cries for help—help for them, sometimes, but many times help for you. Ignoring these signs may cause a lowering of morale and, in most cases, a decrease in productivity.

**WTGB**—Practice being sensitive to your employees' needs.

*Second*, you may have reached a point where your finance person has come to you and said there is not enough cash-flow to pay the payables within the 30-day current status. Many business owners refuse to pay bills until after they reach 30 days. I have been in the presence of some who flat-out refuse to pay any bill until it reaches 60 days. Certain industries even accept it as common practice to not expect payment until 90 days.

There is no excuse for not being able to pay a bill soon after it is received. When you delay it should be as a result of purposeful cash-flow management, not because you do not have the cash.

Most bills are expected and can be budgeted. And if there is a cash-flow problem, maybe it's time to call for help before the payables go from 30 days to 120 past due.

In a situation similar to the one mentioned in the previous paragraphs, upon entering a new client's establishment, the owner's first statement made to us was that she wanted to fire the finance person. She handed us a graph that showed the last fifty-two week's cash-flow. The company had been in a positive cash-flow position for just one week in the last year. The owner blamed the finance person.

When we analyzed the operations of the company, it became very clear that the finance person was actually a prophet. The owner had been bleeding the company dry to pay for the big house, the leased cars, the extravagant trips, the designer clothes, and the Ivy League college education for her son.

She had no education, no management skills, experience, or business knowledge but she "envisioned herself as a manager."

But her worst flaw was that she could not admit she had those shortcomings. Her uncontrolled ego would not allow it. All it knew how to do was spend money. Big money. So that all those around her would think she was successful.

**WTGB**—Always ask, "Who's in control?" Is it you? Or your ego?

We counseled her to seek professional help, place her half-a-million-dollar home on the market, and to turn in the leased cars.

**WTGB**—Ask yourself what your motivation is for acquiring anything new.

*A third indicator* of your possible need for help is that sales are declining or are flat. This is a critical early-warning sign. Most entrepreneurs hesitate to call for help when sales decline or flatten, preferring to affix blame squarely on the economy or their employees. Although the economy can, in some cases, be blamed for deteriorating business profits; unless you have a degree as an economist, it may be wise to consider other reasons your company may have declining sales.

**WTGB**—Don't overreact to waning sales, but do react. Ask questions and listen to the answers.

*A fourth pointer* that you may need help, is when people close to you seem to be always asking you how things are going. If there is a problem, your friends, family, loved-ones can sometimes spot troubles before you see them. They notice more tension in your voice, a decline in your sense of humor, an attitude more fatalistic than usual; you're smoking more, drinking more and swearing more. Listen to their questions—they may be indirectly saying, "Seek help."

*This next gauge* is far more subtle than the other four. It has to do with your approach to your business and your own work ethic. If it is normal for you to have trouble sleeping at night because your mind is continually racing to solve a business problem, it may be time to seek help. If, when you wake in the morning to go to work, you always dread getting out of bed, or better yet, if you frequently end your weekend with the dark thought of what you may face come Monday morning, it may be time to get help. We affectionately refer to this end-of-the-weekend vermin as the Gerb.

The Gerb is a monster that usually appears only on Sunday evenings and the last free evening of your vacation, and is a great predictor of business failure. However, many have learned to live with the Gerb showing up every evening and accept it as part of their life until it's too late. Infant Gerbs show their ugly heads to school kids the evening before exams.

**WTGB**—If the Gerb is attacking you on a frequent basis, you might consider calling for help before it spreads to all of your employees.

*The last sign* to look for is almost too obvious but bears mentioning. If you are constantly saying you are undercapitalized, or if only you could restructure your debt, then you might be better off asking for help from someone who can assist you in correcting the situation that caused your current problem, rather than Band-Aiding the results of your problem.

**WTGB**—Know yourself well enough to realize when to ask for help.

We are in a social system that almost insists on fast results—quick fixes. Sometimes however, the quick fix is but a death sentence for a small business, prolonging the inevitable: complete reorganization under the guidance of a seasoned professional.

The time to call someone for help may be right now. Do not wait until the eleventh hour; it may be too late to dig your business out of the hole. And, by the way, throwing money at a situation might seem right at the time, but in many cases, it's throwing good money after bad.

**WTGB**—Before you throw money at a problem, make sure you understand what the problem is.

So the question remains, why doesn't Larry Ashley ask for help? Why, when it appears all the warning signs are there, does he remain steadfast in his commitment to stay the course? David Harper, Noelle's attorney friend tried to persuade Larry to get some help, but Larry refused to listen. What could we do to wake up Larry? How can he be helped?

**WTGB**—Make a list of all the things with which you feel you need help. Now, place the name of a person who could help you next to each item. Begin meeting each of these people—TODAY.

## Chapter 7

## You Can Lead A Horse to What?

During the course of the last six chapters, we have explored the warning signals of a small business's downward trend and how much of what an owner does or does not do, is not based on sound business judgment, but his uncontrolled ego—his gut reaction. These are the red flags that alert the entrepreneur of imminent business failure.

None of the foregoing is new, however. In fact, this information has been around ever since man began to organize his day in an attempt to better provide a livelihood for himself and his family.

Admittedly, there have never been any records of such alongside the primitive cave-wall pictures of buffalo and antelope drawn by early cave dwellers. But we do know that some individuals who had leadership skills—usually recognized by their, beating-the-life out of their nearest adversaries—took the reins of the tribe, and those with a lesser capacity to inflict personal damage, followed.

Of course, there were always those who chose to go it alone and survived, fending for themselves with their own plot of land, creating a world that provided them with self-sufficiency and minimal dependence on the outside world.

Today, we look at life with a different point of view. The leaders—we now call them presidents—and the independents are the entrepreneurs. And both draw on many parts of society to maintain their existence. And the physical beating of an adversary has pretty much ceased.

So, what if after an entrepreneur is confronted with all the warning signals, he refuses to respond and take the corrective steps to halt the rapid demise of his company? Why when all the signs are there, and the prophets standing around the water cooler are screaming at the top of their lungs, is the entrepreneur deaf, dumb, and blind?

Why when it is so easy to read a business journal, the local newspaper, a business magazine, or talk to a business advisor; do some entrepreneurs continue to do it "their way"—even when it so clear that "their way" is what has gotten them into the predicament in the first place?

**Can you really lead a horse to water?**

What magic do some small business consultants have that provides them with an almost 100% success ratio in turning companies around? Whereas with others, the company reverts back to being in trouble within a year after they leave.

Is it that some business advisors are better than others? Maybe. But our experience indicates that most business advisors are credible, and if the entrepreneur follows the plan that has been devised, he/she will become more profitable.

So why do some entrepreneurs ignore the advice of their employees, friends, and counsels?

Remember earlier, we mentioned the independent caveman who went off on his own and provided for his family. Hunting for deer, coming back with a raccoon, and hoping his spouse could make it edible, at least for the kids, was not too complicated. I did not say it wasn't difficult, just not that complicated.

When he started out, he was an entrepreneur providing for his family. Then his family grew and what happened? His obligations grew. He could not do it all on his own so he had to recruit his sons and daughters.

Recruiting back then was much simpler. You just said something like, "Martin, you plow the lower thirty today and Sarah will slop the hogs." The response was usually, "Yes, sir."

But the key here was that the ancient entrepreneur realized his limitations and began to rely on others to help in the running of the business. The successful ones never looked back and didn't second-guess their employees. Some of you may be thinking that the independent caveman really did not have a business, but I can find no more challenging and complicated a business than that of running a family. And when one person attempts to go it alone, the job is many times overwhelming.

So why can't modern-day entrepreneurs divest themselves of some of their responsibilities and move ahead as the ancient caveman did?

For the simple reason that they are the sum product of all they have experienced from the beginnings of their lives, including the results of their genetic makeup. They are caught in a vortex of invisible pressures and forces they cannot see, hear, smell, taste, or touch.

Somewhere deep within them is a hidden room. A room with pulsing tentacles that stretch out in all directions and touch every portion of their mind. The room is seething with past images, words, phrases, punishments, rebukes, and disappointments that flow out the feelers and infect every bit of the entrepreneurial decision-making process.

**WTGB**—You are not a simple, but a complex human being. All your reactions are learned and/or are a result of your perspective—your viewpoint.

And where does all this baggage originate? Life. Well, maybe not life, but people in your life. We are all born with a positive self-image. Think about it. What in a baby's mind cannot be accomplished? Every child thinks he can fly! Where does that come from?

But throughout childhood, the image begins to

deteriorate. It may begin at home with an angry word from a parent—not intended to harm the child, but remember, parents only know how to parent by the example they had when they were growing up. Then friends begin to chip away at your self-image: a snide remark, a tease, a criticism, a punch, a push.

Then your teachers and coaches: "Can't you catch anything? Can't you see the basket? Can't you see the board? Can't you understand English? That question is stupid. That decision was stupid. You're stupid."

Teachers, sometimes, transfer their own hang-ups, prejudices and inadequacies to their students. This helps the teacher feel better about himself, but causes untold damage to the students. There are countless stories that people could tell you about the scars they carry from an encounter with a teacher.

Unfortunately, this type of interaction continues throughout your whole life. So, as a protective mechanism, after your positive self-image has been destroyed and been replaced by a poor self-image, your ego takes up a position as a sentry.

You navigate through life doing the best you can to avoid feeling worse about yourself. You do whatever it takes to survive, even drive your company into bankruptcy to protect your poor self-image. You relinquish control to your ego, and it shows no mercy.

So what can be done?

The small-business owner must become introspective

and delve deep within the recesses of his or her mind to uncover his/her motivations for all decisions that are made or not made. A *Self Enlightenment.*

And if self-analysis is not your thing, then seek out someone who can help you uncover your weaknesses. This person may take the form of a friend, a minister, a priest, a spouse, or a stranger. In any case, to think that you can solve your problem alone, is to think wrong. Sometimes you need someone to listen to you talk about yourself, your fears, your aspirations, so that you can hear them.

**WTGB**—"No man is an island, entire of itself...." John Donne 1572—1631

The problem is that your prejudices and idiosyncrasies could be the result of deep-down scars that are still oozing a poison that threatens to infect you for the rest of your life. It's like driving into the sun all the time. If that was the only way you saw life, you would miss all the beauty and intensity of the colors in the world.

That's what an uncontrolled ego does. It washes out the vibrant colors and masks them in a haze of fear, anger, and mistrust.

**WTGB**—Operating with an uncontrolled ego is like trying to live in a commune with a rabid wolf as a pet.

So the only way to turn your business around may be to seek counseling. Personal, psychological counseling. Not group therapy. One on one with a trained professional. Private individuals have been seeking help in weeding out gremlins for years. And some of these individuals have owned companies. Some have owned large corporations.

But the end result of their internal exploration only led to one thing—success. They were able to overcome the echoes in their heads and to move forward with their business goals; trusting their staff to do their jobs; accepting that they couldn't do everything themselves and that they might not be the best person to talk to that certain customer, or make that decision, or purchase the next shipment of products. And they accepted advice and followed it.

But even better, after solving their internal turmoil, they ended up happier at work, at home, and inside their minds. You may have a couple of hang-ups that are holding you back from achieving real stability and success with your company.

Very rarely is there a business owner who likes all that has to be done to operate the company. Some like sales but hate the accounting; some like the accounting but hate making the collection calls; some like developing the new products but hate writing up the documentation.

If you cannot bring yourself to do all the aspects, or if you realize that you are not the best person for the job, then you must turn those responsibilities over to those who are more suited to carry out those functions.

**WTGB**—Take an aggressive approach to covering the areas that make you uncomfortable. Recognize them and deal with them.

# Chapter 8

# Focus Focus, Who's Got the Focus?

"We won't quit until every car is sold!" yelled the manager to his sales team. He wasn't angry. He was excited. He was motivating his salesmen to get out there and make sales. He was focused, and he wanted his employees to be focused.

But what if they were confused about what they were supposed to do with their time? How many cars would get sold? Not as many as if they were focused.

Focus, or the lack there of, is just as much a business problem as having no sales or poor cash-flow. But as with all business problems, the lack of focus is the result of a much bigger problem. So let's explore why certain business entrepreneurs can't find their focus.

## What is focus?

It seems a simple enough question. To the automobile sales manager, it is to sell cars.

Athletes are masters at staying focused. They will even use the term when describing what they must do as they approach a challenge. They will admit the need to stay focused, and at the end of their trial, if they have failed, they'll attribute it to not staying focused. Staying focused means keeping the image, the goal, the prize clearly in your sights—in your visual or mental sights.

We falter when our goal is not in focus or we are not focused on our goal.

So why can't some small-business owners stay focused? Some don't even start out focused. What causes lack of focus? The forest for the trees? Possibly. But why is it that some business owners just have to be everything to their clients or customers? The old Jack-of-all-trades. And they think their business has to provide all the client's needs. Even in areas where there is no profitable experience.

Let's say you have the capability of performing one or two services really well, but the economy, so you think, forces you to take on everything you can just to keep your staff occupied and cash flowing through the company. The problem with that scenario is that sooner or later the short side of the profit margin will catch up with the growing payables.

A while ago we worked with a client who wrestled

with this problem almost on a weekly basis. We assisted our client in preparing a proposal for a national corporation and the price we suggested to perform his service was 28% higher than what our client had learned a competitor was offering for the same service.

The first reaction of our client was to drop his price to meet his competition. After three hours of going over the numbers, it was proved to him that he could not make enough money to pay the employees, support them in the field, and cover the current office overhead if he decreased price.

He finally realized that if he had any hope at all of closing the deal, he would have to sell his price to the national company on his company's reputation and the quality of his service record.

He won the contract—not without some concessions—but he made a profit, and learned a valuable lesson. We weren't convinced however that he wouldn't again try to drop his price when the occasion arose.

For years, rather than losing a job and having to lay off a couple of people for a week or two to keep the company healthy, he had chosen to place the company income into a deficit position so that over time, having stayed with that same philosophy—which got him into the fix he was now in—the company would go bankrupt.

He didn't stay focused on what he was supposed to do: making sure the business was profitable. Instead he wanted to make sure his employees liked him.

**WTGB**-It is great to be liked by your employees, but it should never be your prime motivation. Keep the company healthy, your workers employed, and if they like you, all the better.

What if the inventor of the piano, back in 1709-Bartotomeo Cristofori of Florence, Italy—made all the notes sound together when you pressed down any key? What if the inventor of the flashlight back in 1891—The Bristol Electric Lamp Co. of England—decided that the beam of light should be diffused instead of concentrated?

What if, when you started school, you were taught every subject all at once, including graduate courses in nuclear physics?

The primary word here is focus. The flashlight's rays focus into a beam. One key plays one unique note (if the piano is in tune) and in third grade you were taught a different curriculum than in your third year of college. So, if everything else seems to be focused, why can't some small business owners stay focused?

## How do you maintain your focus?

Your business plan. You know, that elusive, black-bound, soft-cover book you authored when you tried to borrow money for your business from the bank. They asked you for a business plan, so with great anxiety you struggled to put together on paper the vision you had in your head.

Some business owners have never written a business

plan. It is not that they couldn't, it is just that they either did not believe in it, or they thought it was too time-consuming to complete.

You need to force yourself to write a business plan.

Once you commit something to paper, where your eyes can see it and your mind can read it, the conscious mind communicates the knowledge to the subconscious mind and magic happens. When you write it down, your subconscious mind pushes your conscious mind thus causing you to act. You miraculously begin to do the things necessary to make your declarations come true.

A person who never makes a list of the things he wishes to accomplish in a given day, may oscillate through the day accomplishing very little, only finishing those items on a hit-or-miss basis. And so it goes with a person's career, life, or business.

Taking the time to write down your goals is a simple way of beginning a business plan. But then comes the discipline to complete it and then follow it.

Operating without a business plan is like sailing a ship without a rudder, or being on a trip without a map, or singing a song with no definite melody, or going fishing without some sort of bait, or lending money with no repayment plan, or raising a family with no rules, or living with no purpose.

Operating a business without a business plan is most assuredly business suicide.

**WTGB**-Start your plan today. Jot down your ideas and dreams. Make lists. Draw diagrams.

Without a business plan, your focus is blurred. Your direction is not clear. Your ability to maximize your energy in the most profitable areas is diminished. Without a business plan, you have no way of keeping on track. It is like taking a trip across country in your car with your family. For three weeks, maybe three months, you plan. You make mileage measurements, make hotel reservations, check out scenic stops along the way, make appointments with longtime friends, and alert relatives.

Then the day you are to take off, just before you leave, you open your bureau drawer and casually throw in the maps, reservation confirmation numbers, friends' and relatives' phone numbers, and all the travel brochures. You then hop in the car, turn to the family and say, "Boy are we going to have a great time."

Fat chance. You've most likely learned from your father and mother, that the success of a trip is in the planning. And the more what-iffing you do, the more likely your trip will be smooth. Of course the chances you'll think of everything are very slim. And invariably, something unexpected will happen.

Now my father was a planner. So was my mother. I remember a trip across the country to California. We arrived at the "Last Chance for Gas" before the desert that separates Arizona from California civilization. It was the planned place both my parents decided we would get gas—we didn't want to run out on the desert—we'd potty ourselves, and fill our jug with water. We also arrived just after sunset, so the ride across such a dry flat expanse would not only be cooler, but the sun would not be in our eyes.

There were three of us kids. Three boys. My mother miraculously stayed out of a mental institution. But we were crossing the desert. You know—hot, dry, sand, snakes, cactus, dry, tumble weed, dry—very dry. About thirty minutes out, the three of us kids were dying of thirst. So we opened up the water jug and almost keeled over.

***Sulfur Water! Yuck!*** The only way we could drink it was to hold our noses. Even the best planning didn't foresee this obstacle.

By not having a business plan, or writing one and then throwing it in a drawer, is one of the most deadly things you can do. You're killing your business along with your livelihood and the income of all your employees. You're forcing failure. You're planning it. And you are not staying focused.

**WTGB**-Practice staying focused. When you begin to drift, catch yourself and get back on course.

1) Make up a reminder list and read it every day. Post it somewhere so you can see it easily.

2) Make up signs in your work area with key words to keep you thinking in a certain direction.

Read positive-attitude books. They can usually be found in the self-help section of your bookstore.

## Chapter 9

## But I Can't Follow the Plan!

Dennis Yung followed the neatly dressed woman past the small offices to the large wooden door at the end of the hall. Mrs. Dodd knocked twice and opened it.

"Tom, this is Dennis, he's with the new bank, Don'tcha Wanna Trust and Deposit Co.," Tom Langstrom's executive assistant said.

"Come on in, Dennis. I appreciate you stopping by so soon," Tom said, extending his hand.

"Well, Tom, after you saw my boss at the Chamber meeting Wednesday evening, he came in Thursday morning and told me you expressed an interest in expanding your business."

Tom Langstrom, president of WashMore, Inc., took his place behind the modern pedestal desk, leaned back in his leather chair and said, "That's right. Have a seat. We plan to expand and take on a whole new territory."

Dennis Yung sat down and said, "We'd be glad to help you."

"That's great; I'll need about $145,000 to get this project off the ground."

"Okay, Tom. I see you get right to the point, so I'll get to the point, too. Can I see your business plan?" Dennis asked as he settled into the soft-cushioned chair.

"Certainly," Tom said as he reached into the top drawer of his credenza that sat beneath the window behind his desk.

After a few minutes of watching Tom search, Dennis broke the silence. "You want me to come back for it?"

"I know it's here somewhere. Alice," he called out.

"Yes, Mr. Langstrom?" Alice Dodd asked as she reentered the office of her boss of seven years.

"Where's our business plan?" Tom asked, standing behind his desk, an exasperated look on his face.

"What business plan? I didn't know we had one," Alice blurted out.

**WTGB**—If you have a business plan, it should be where you can readily get your hands on it.

So where is *your* business plan? Remember, you were trying to secure the necessary funding to get your business off the ground. The bank required a business plan back then, and you went through the motions. Why can't you find it? Why haven't you been using it and updating it as your business aged?

**WTGB**—A business plan is a living document.

Maybe it is because all you did was go through the motions. You didn't believe in the plan in the first place. Maybe you didn't take it seriously. Maybe you hate rules, structure, restrictions—you're the boss, you can do whatever you want. Right?

But, it is up to you to set the mood, the philosophy, the pace, the standard of excellence, and the commitment. You are the leader, and the leader is under a microscope. And it is "follow-the-leader" out there. Your employees do as you do. So if you do not follow a plan, neither will they.

But why don't you believe in a business plan?

Well, one reason might be that you do not believe in planning, or you feel you don't need to plan on paper. And the only reason you wrote a business plan in the first place was because you were forced to by your bank. Besides, you know how to run a business. Your father ran one for years, and he didn't have a written business plan. You keep your plan in your head like he did.

I admire people who can keep everything in their heads instead of writing them down. I cannot rely on my mind to recall things when I need them, so I resort to making lists. But I personally know many people who pride themselves on never writing anything down. Of course, I am always reminding them when we are going to have a meeting, or when they have to pay a certain bill, or make a call for a sale. But they don't use up any paper.

Maybe another reason why you don't use a business plan is that you hate following rules. And a business plan is just one more rule you don't need. It's just one more inhibition to operating your business the way you want. That is one of the reasons why you started your own business—to be independent—reporting to no one.

Let's face it, one of the main reasons you went into business for yourself was to be out from under someone else's thumb—away from rules. Boy, did *you* get into business for the wrong reason. Yes, you do have the freedom to work or not to work on a certain day. But you had that before. You say you'd get fired if you didn't show up for work. Not work enough days and you will end up firing yourself from your own business.

**WTGB**—When you own your own business, of all the company's employees, you have the most rules to follow. And if you think you don't, then you'd better start looking for a job.

Conformity is difficult for many. But sometimes nonconformity is detrimental to your business heath, especially if it leads to financial losses because of a decision you made based on gut feelings rather than sound business logic.

Choosing not to follow a business plan can cause falling-profits disease: inflammation of the payables, decrease in the recommended daily percentage of sales, irritation of the personnel pool, and restricted flow of receivables—all curable, but sometimes only through repeated injections of logic or through a more radical treatment such as closing the business.

In all these circumstances, it is not the business plan that could save a business, but the continual revisiting of the business plan and adjusting the operating procedures of the company to accomplish the goals of the business plan.

**WTGB**—Continually revisit your business plan.

Once, we had the unpleasant task of following a long line of advisors brought in to help turnaround a business that was too far gone. The owner had developed a beautiful business plan, but had not spent one once of energy following it or taking it out of the drawer to review it. It was actually a fairly decent strategy.

The purpose of the plan was to secure $125,000 from the bank to provide for the purchase of additional equipment and the expense of moving to a new location. It took into consideration the needed increase in sales to meet the debt service and solved that problem by showing the hiring of another sales person.

What it didn't show was how the sales person was to generate the sales, and from where the sales would come. Also, the owner, to whom the sales person was to report, knew nothing about setting sales goals, tracking sales, sales analysis, or managing and motivating a sales person.

Suddenly, she found herself in a real fix. Her sales were down, and her payables were up. The salesman she had hired was not producing (of course he had no hard-and-fast quota). The bank was getting nervous, and so were her creditors.

And although all the signs were there that she should take the time to revisit her plan and make adjustments to bring her method of operating back in line, she turned her back on her staff, her Small Business Development Center advisor, and her consulting company, and proceeded to do it her way.

She had never run a business before, but her father had. She figured she would show her father and become just as successful.

**WTGB**—Make sure you start and operate a business for the right reasons.

Sadly, she had to close her company and declare personal bankruptcy. We placed some of the blame for her demise on the bank that lent her the money. They had a copy of the business plan and it clearly showed that the strategic sales portion of the process was not addressed, and the owner's personal resume showed a complete lack of sales experience.

She had been an account executive for a radio station. Not the same as going out and making cold calls, trying to incite interest in a marketing company.

The client blamed everyone else but herself for her failure. No one knew anything. She had some big problems that stemmed from her relationship with her father. He never accepted her because he wanted a son. She was always running in a deficit-affection position. No love. No interest. No positive self-esteem.

Her self-image was based on what her father thought of her—and he never gave her a second thought. And so her ego grew to be as large as the big outdoors—and out of control.

**WTGB**—If you are going to run a business, you

absolutely need a business plan.

The next absolutely is that you need to continually review your plan and adjust your methods and styles to meet your goals. Or you must adjust your goals.

On the upside of stories, there is a company recently contracted that has been operating for five years run by two enterprising women who agonized over their business plan when they decided to develop a partnership and embark on their entrepreneurial voyage.

They continually review the plan and remind each other why they started the business, what products and services they are to offer, and where they are to offer them. They frequently receive calls from businesses that are located out of the geographic area within which they planned to operate.

And time and again, they refuse this new business because they revisit their business plan, a plan that analyzed their costs of operating out of the area and helped them draw an imaginary line in the sand. They never cross over the line. They could, but if they do, they know that their ability to perform and still make a reasonable profit is diminished.

This business responsibility has now become second nature, and their business is strong and growing.

If you don't have a board of directors, then who keeps you on track? Your business plan will help you stay focused. But it won't if you hide it away in a drawer.

**WTGB**—Keep your plan out in plain view. Make a special place for it.

# Chapter 10

# An Entrepreneurial Day

To help the aspiring entrepreneur focus on his or her strengths, many career and business advisors administer all sorts of tests. These tests are important in order to find a pattern that may or may not suggest a person's success or failure as an entrepreneur.

There may be however, certain qualities needed by an entrepreneur such as: discipline, persistence, honesty, integrity, ethics, creativity, strength of self-image that are missed by these series of questions.

All these items need to be weighed as an integral part of the whole of an entrepreneur. But instead of spouting off long sentences of theory and philosophy, why don't we follow an entrepreneur around for a day of two?

**Monday Morning:**
6:00 AM—The alarm rings. Now, our representative

entrepreneur works out of her home, so after making a pot of coffee, cleaning up last night's mess, spending fifteen minutes meditating, she is at her desk in her sweats by 7:00 AM.

7:00 AM-8:30 AM—This time is spent recapping last Friday's activities, the previous week's activities, and reviewing the plan for the day and the rest of the week.

8:30 AM-11:30 AM—Our entrepreneur spends the morning reviewing her last week's research of new markets to infiltrate. She prioritizes her findings based on her knowledge and prospect of potential sales. She enters the weekend's new contacts into her computer and schedules phone calls to these new potential customers for later in the week.

11:30 AM-1:00 PM—This time is spent away from the office, usually running to the bank to make a deposit or to lunch with a business prospect or an associate—never a friend. (Time for getting properly dressed is also included in this time slot. A business suit or appropriate professional attire—not jeans or braless. The image of success needs to be communicated at all times. Make sure you always carry your business cards.)

1:00 PM-6:00 PM—She reserves this time for client work. Monday is <u>not</u> a good day to be making sales calls, so working on her client projects is the best use of this time slot.

6:00 PM-7:00 PM—This time is spent reviewing mail, sending faxes, forming letters, and printing and mailing them.

7:00 PM-8:30 PM—She has dinner while reading industry magazines—marking pertinent articles regarding past, current, or future client work, as well as highlighting personal business information to advance her own company.

8:30 PM-9:00 PM—It's time to clean up the dinner dishes and straighten up the house.

9:00 PM-10:00 PM—She reads the evening paper online, saving pertinent articles to organized computer files pertaining to client work, personal and business growth, client names, and businesses mentioned in the news. She also scans the social media pages for news.

10:00 PM-11:30 PM—She's reading a book on the latest business techniques.

11:30 PM-11:45 PM—She gets ready for bed.

11:45 PM-ZZZZZ (or read for pleasure until ZZZZZ).

## **Tuesday Morning:**

7:00 AM-8:30 AM—Review the plan for the day. Make adjustments to the week's goals as necessary. Write letters. Send out emails.

8:30 AM-11:30 AM—She calls to connect with new clients, new prospects, and new businesses. Tuesday morning, her prospective clients are in a better and more receptive mood after the trauma of Monday is behind them.

11:30 AM-12:30 PM—She works through lunch at her desk. She is still in conversations with potential clients or centers of influence.

12:30 PM-5:30 PM—This time is spent making calls, having meetings and conferences with clients, prospects, centers of influence. Then there are more calls, reviews of past potential client conversations, review of the Chamber book to jog her memory for anyone else to call, page by page reviews of the local phone book to jog her memory of people with whom to connect.

5:30 PM-7:00 PM—Our entrepreneur prepares to attend her local Chamber of Commerce meeting. Once again, she wears proper business attire and remembers to bring her business cards.

7:00 PM-8:30 PM—She attends the Chamber meeting and exchanges business cards.

8:30 PM-9:00 PM—She engages in a few conversations with new contacts.

9:00 PM-9:30 PM—This time is reserved for the drive home.

9:30 PM-11:30 PM—see Monday

**And it starts all over again.**

This particular entrepreneur is working sixteen hours a day. By the time Friday evening rolls around, she will have put in eighty hours. Saturday morning will be devoted to preparing client billings, her own business's bookkeeping, and tying up any loose ends from the week.

Saturday afternoon she has to cut the lawn and do the wash. She forces herself to relax Saturday evening, attend church Sunday morning, and relax Sunday afternoon. She falls asleep in her chair by 9:30 Sunday evening, wakes up at 11:30, walks down the hall, sets the alarm for 6:00 AM, and crawls into bed.

What the tests don't ask you is: How long can you maintain your enthusiasm, drive, and persistence working eighty hours a week, week after week, sometimes going well over a year before getting seven consecutive days off?

This one question, unasked, launches many novice entrepreneurs into a black hole of misconception. Many choose to become self-employed because they cannot continue being strapped to their jobs, only to find out they are even more enslaved.

**WTGB**—When you begin a new business or buy a business, it is common to spend long hours and long weeks learning the ropes and building your business. But it's worth it.

I would not have room to tell you all the stories I have been told of people moving to one of the southern coastal communities to open a business and be by the water, only to close up shop within nine months because they never had time to go to the beach.

Whether in the north or the south, operating a

business is the same. If you want to be successful, you have to put in the hours and be disciplined. And this is where many business owners become discouraged.

The daily business-life of an entrepreneur is anything but glamorous. And the freedom that is won from not having to report to a boss is transferred to the constraints of conscience, which is a many-times-more demanding taskmaster.

But what do you need to know to become an entrepreneur?

I've only met one man who absolutely was at peace with his business and thoroughly enjoyed all aspects of his Entrepreneurship. It was during the summer of 1990. We took the family to Florida for vacation.

He ran an umbrella, chair, and boogie-board rental service out of the back of a truck parked in the sand at Daytona Beach. Every day he showed up at 10:00 AM and folded up shop at 5:30 PM.

Now, I knew he didn't work all year at this because I had been there in the off-season and he was never there. I asked him what he did to make money during the late fall, winter, and early spring. He said he made about $48,000 net in the summer and watched football the rest of the year.

I felt a sharp pain in my stomach.

He knew his limitations. He confessed that he couldn't manage people well. So he didn't. He said he couldn't sell, so he sat and waited for the public to come to him. He admitted he was lazy, and loved to watch football. He had a great tan. He absolutely knew himself.

**WTGB**—"Know Thyself."—Diogenes Laertius (200ca)

The first thing you need to know is yourself. Our Daytona entrepreneur knew himself. He knew what he liked and did not like. He knew what he was good at and what he wasn't. And he did not work at something that dictated he change his psyche. He did not want to learn how to be a salesman, or how to manage people, so he developed a service that fit his ego and his lifestyle.

You need to be honest about your flaws and your weaknesses. You need to admit when you need help in certain areas, and be willing to change. And if you have never been on your own before, and you have always reported to a boss, watch out!

**WTGB**—In your attempt to hit the ground running as an entrepreneur, you may find the ground already moving faster than you can run.

**WTGB**—The psychological make-up of the entrepreneur determines the success of a business more than any other factor.

Can the entrepreneur maintain the drive, the stamina, the long-distance run by himself? Can the entrepreneur believe strongly enough in her idea to sustain criticism, setbacks, disappointments? Can the entrepreneur clearly see his shortcomings and gather around himself those persons who can help him grow his idea into a reality?

Knowing the answers to these questions is more critical than securing funding for the business. Not every idea is going to be funded by a local bank or venture-capital company. And it will never be funded without a business plan. But that is not your biggest problem.

You may wonder if any of our new entrepreneurial clients ever fail. The answer to that is yes, many do. Because the entrepreneur could not, or chose not to, continue because he became discouraged.

**WTGB**—Every night, after you crawl into bed, read a page or so of a positive motivational book. <u>You Can if You Think You Can</u> by Norman Vincent Peale is a good place to start.

Many entrepreneurs become discouraged because the business plan took too long to create, because the business plan was too complicated, because the sales side of their business escaped them, because they didn't like processing checks and entering data into the computer, because the bank refused to grant them a loan.

They become discouraged because they are now working for $7.00 an hour and their last job paid them $15.00 an hour.

And many of them cannot discipline themselves to work the sixteen hours a day, or if they do put in that kind of time, they don't know how to prioritize each function based on its maximum rate of return.

**WTGB**—If you break down each facet of your business into smaller parts, the whole process becomes more manageable.

## Chapter 11

## Does the Hat Fit?

I'm sure you have seen movies, TV programs, and commercials showing the man who answers the phone of his one-person company. The customer at the other end of the phone asks for purchasing and he says, "just a moment," places the caller on hold, waits a few seconds and then picks it up and says, "purchasing."

Then the customer wants to talk to someone in customer service, and he goes through the same routine, changing his voice slightly to vary the sound, giving the impression that the company is fully staffed.

As an entrepreneur, you must become accustomed to wearing a variety of hats. Sometimes it is culture-shock to go from being the head of a division in a large corporation to running the whole show in your own small business including cleaning the toilets.

But what types of hats can you expect to wear?

Well, there is the sales hat, the finance hat, the marketing hat, the advertising hat, the operations hat, the management hat, the manufacturing hat, the R & D hat, the funding hat, the personnel hat, the maintenance hat and a few more.

When you begin as an entrepreneur, you must realize that it is all up to you. As you embark on this new adventure, you have to do everything and be able to wear all of the hats.

Then, as your business grows or—better said—in order for your business to grow, you must be willing to pass off some of those hats to someone else who is better equipped or qualified to wear them. But initially, you will have to wear all the hats unless you have enough venture capital available to hire the people you need from day one.

So, now that we have determined that you have to wear a number of hats, we need to figure out when, where, and for how long you should wear these hats. Take for instance the sales hat. No, let's start with the finance hat. No, let's concentrate on the manufacturing hat… no, the marketing… no the advertising.

And that is what happens. That is the thought process that goes on inside the head of the novice entrepreneur. He/she cannot determine which hat should be worn first and for how long. And the fear of making a mistake causes the entrepreneur to spend weeks, months, sometimes years spinning wheels, going in circles, unable to head in the proper direction. No pun intended.

**WTGB**—Doing nothing will assure your place at the end of the line.

You must be willing to make the mistakes, and hopefully your correct decisions will outweigh the wrong ones. Of course, you can pad the correct choices in your favor by doing a certain amount of homework before making those selections.

In any case, let us try to set our fears aside and tackle one aspect at a time.

**WTGB**—Surround yourself with positive messages. Use your wall, desk, and notebook.

### Product/Service Hat

You must have a clear understanding of the product or service you are offering. Whatever the product or service, the first hat you have to wear is that of a devil's advocate. Who is going to buy this product or service? Where and what is the market for your idea?

And do not be fooled by the Internet. Many have invested thousands and set up their own WebPages. "I get 10,000 hits a week," they boast. But no sales. The little kids and the teenagers on their home computers are dancing all over the wires, but they are not serious consumers.

You are probably not the best person to play devil's advocate, so you need to find others who will help you gain an understanding of the value of your idea. Try strangers. Friends will like it because they like you. You need honesty, not sympathy.

**WTGB**—Don't be afraid of the truth, it will help you succeed.

Along with helping people turn their companies around, we continually attempt to assist fledgling entrepreneurs in their quests to start businesses. All our clients come from referrals. That helps us weed out those who want to walk to the end of the dock and just dangle their feet in the water. Usually by the time we begin with a new entrepreneur, he/she is 100% ready to make the emotional and financial commitments.

Some time ago we had a partnership come to us and enlist our services to assist them in launching their newly-patented product. It was an ingeniously simple device, and we saw the hunger in their eyes.

But one of the partners, the one who took on the role of salesman, didn't know the first thing about sales and would not admit it. He would go out and speak to people and his enthusiasm would give him the verbal responses he was looking for, but never the sales he needed.

His potential customers did not comprehend the owner-benefits of purchasing his product. And he didn't know how to ask for the order. The only thing his potential customers saw was hype.

We tried to steer him in the direction of a sales-training course, but we needed to break through something else that was holding him back.

Eventually, at a one-on-one session in his home, he broke down crying and told us that six years ago he lost his business and had to declare bankruptcy. He got over his head in a rental-space obligation in a local shopping mall and his sales didn't provide enough cash flow. A review of his pricing structure revealed that he was very reasonable, but too low to afford the image he was trying to portray.

So why was the image so important? And could that be his problem? It sure was. And the fact that his wife held a high profile job and earned a good salary contributed to his poor feelings about his self-worth even though she and their children loved him.

We struggled with him for about three months, but could not get him to take any sales courses. The business is no longer operating.

\*\*\*

Okay, so let's say you have tested the waters, and your idea seems to be a good one. Now comes the question, "Is there a market?"

A famous company, that will go unnamed, decided that it needed to revamp its complete dog food line from the logo to the packaging to the formula. Thousands of dollars were spent making everything just right. The product was put on the shelves and after six months it was confirmed that the new dog food wasn't selling as well as the old.

The company executives assumed that if they enhanced the formula with additional nutrients and not worry about the taste, because they thought dogs would eat anything, they would be safe. But they did not test the food on the dogs. Turns out, the dogs hated it.

**WTGB**—Make sure you identify and test your market.

It may be necessary to hire a market-research firm to help you. If you do not have the funds, you will have to do the marketing yourself. Start by checking out how many other companies are offering the same service you intend to provide. And, if there is no one selling this service, you have to ask yourself, why not?

We had a client who was hell-bent on providing a service that no one in Western New York was selling. We kept asking him why no one else offered it. It became very clear why: The cost of providing it was way above what any company would pay for that kind of service. Customers were better off doing the work themselves. It was an expensive lesson for our client to learn.

But let us say your service or product has passed a tough marketing analysis and you are convinced you really have a good idea. Now you need to get that idea into the minds of others who will readily part with their money to acquire that product or service you offer.

### The Sales Hat

Sales. The word alone strikes fear in the hearts of even the most formidable entrepreneur. Without sales however, there is no business, no product or service moves, and no money is exchanged. There is no profit. Without sales, there is no entrepreneur. So there has to be a sales effort. And, as an entrepreneur, either *you* have to do the selling or you'll have to hire someone to do it for you. For now, let us assume you do not have the financial where-with-all to hire someone.

How do you sell your product or service?

The best way, if you are broke and operating on a shoe-string, is to learn how to network. The more people you can expose to your offerings, the more will know about you and your product and the more chances you will have to make a sale. Tell them what you do, that you need to make three sales this week, and that you need help. Magic happens.

People like to help, and if you ask them for help, they will find a way to help you and always ask how you are doing every time they see you. Tell your story as in chapter 4.

You need to become accustomed to going to network gatherings. Many are free, and if there is a cost, it is usually minimal. And it can be viewed as a business expense.

You should learn to read the paper searching for names you know. We tell our clients to even read the bridal pages in the Sunday paper. Our male clients balk at first, but then they invariably come back to us the next week and say a buddy they hadn't seen in six years just got married. And, of course the write-up always states where the bride and groom are employed.

Our response is: call him up and congratulate him. Then, when he asks, tell him what you are doing and ask him to refer you to someone else, who might know someone else, and on and on.

**WTGB**—Send out five letters a day or five emails, and make a point of trying to identify three new people to whom you can expose your business.

## Chapter 12

## A Balancing Act

One of the most common dilemmas of business ownership of any size, is keeping all the facets of the company in balance. In other words, where do you place your emphasis this hour, today, this week, this month, or this year and how? Is it in finance, sales, management, or marketing?

There is almost an art to making sure all the aspects of a business operates in a cohesive, juxtaposed rhythm—where sales continues generating enough revenue to cover expenses; where management smoothes over the staff when overtime is needed to meet a deadline; where finance provides for a positive cash-flow in spite of increased supply costs.

Some business owners try to control all these areas by themselves. They sell, make the bank deposits, supervise the line work, run the marketing meetings, order inventory, go to the post office, and even open the mail.

Having said all that, we are not really going to address the act of balancing the components of an ongoing business, but there is something that lurks, festers, grows in dark corners, and jumps out at you when you least expect it. It spins you around, causing you to make wrong decisions even when the right decision is staring you in the face.

*It is the balance of your company's potential growth against your mental state of mind.*

**WTGB**—Concentrate on being sensitive to those around you, and place your needs last.

Many times in analyzing a business, it is discovered that the owner or president of the ailing company is missing a key ingredient, and has replaced it with another much poorer substitute: a positive mindset has been replaced with an aggressive self-set. And in reverse, a growing company is almost always led by an owner with a strong positive self-image.

Here is an example of how an incorrect mindset can cause your business to lose money.

Let us say that your office manager has informed you she thinks the pricing structure of your product is out of step with the reality of your business profitability. In fact, she tells you that you are losing money. The solution is not as clear as you might think. You would assume all you have to do is raise prices.

But in order to properly affix the correct price to a product, you must take into consideration a number of factors:
1. What is the current cost of raw materials?
2. What does it cost to manufacture the product?
3. What price will the market bear?
4. What price would a customer pay for your particular product or service?

We are not going to dwell at all on the costs of goods sold or the weighted factor of your overhead on the pricing structure. What we are going to discuss is why, after the pricing is calculated, taking into consideration all the particulars of fixing a price, do some business owners refuse to stand firm with their fees and insist on giving the store away, granting discounts and cutting numerous deals?

"I'm afraid the sales will drop," one client said.
Our response was, "We hope sales do drop."

He nearly choked at our response. But truth is, if he kept selling his services at his current prices, it would only be a matter of a year before he would be out of business. If sales decreased, his losses would decrease. But of course, he would still go out of business unless he addressed the real problem.

**WTGB**—You don't have to make every sale, just the ones that lead to profits.

How do you know if your prices are too low? A good indication is that if you do not have a salesperson, you are only losing fifteen to twenty percent of the business to your competitors. Without a salesperson, you should be losing roughly 60% of the business to your competitors.

The salesperson can move the percentage down. But, if you have no sales staff, and you are capturing a substantial percentage of the market, something is wrong with your prices, especially if you do not have enough money to pay the bills and your income and expense statement is in a loss position.

So, if your office manager has come to you and shows you she determined the new pricing of your service, taking in consideration a survey of your competitors, why would you have trouble accepting the new prices?

And by the way, if you are the only salesperson in the company and you do not believe in the prices, neither will your customers.

So, what is preventing you from using the new pricing?

One answer may be the fear of rejection. Somewhere in your past you experienced a devastating rejection—a "no," maybe long ago from your father or mother in response to something you thought you did right but resulted in a reprimand. Maybe you were told flat out, "You're stupid."

Maybe your best friend walked by your lemonade stand and laughed out loud at the price of your lemonade. And even though you were doing well, your friend's laugh scarred you forever.

Maybe the company you used to work for was so price-conscious, with customers only interested in the lowest prices, that mindset has bled over into your current style of business operation.

Another explanation is that maybe you just want everyone to like you, so you cut everyone a deal. Or maybe you don't think your service is worth the price your office manager wants you to charge.

**WTGB**—The next time you feel like giving a customer a break in the price, ask yourself why you are doing it. Unless it will ultimately add additional revenue to your business by encouraging a larger sales volume from that customer, maybe you had better reconsider.

Some years back, we had a client who was looking to retire from his job as a reservationist at a national airline company. He spent his entire day answering the phone and interrogating the reservation computer system for the cheapest fares for the company's customers. Call after call would come in with basically only two criteria: *When can I get there, and how much will it cost?*

For almost thirty years he had it drummed into his head by the demands of the customers who called him that price was the determining factor. So when he began to embark on his own career (he was a designer—and a very good one) he continually under-priced his competition, underselling his talent and expertise.

His weekends were full of shows, and his evenings brought private sessions. But when his costs were set against his gross sales, he did not make enough to even pay himself a salary. If it were not for his spouse who owned her own business, he would have lost his house, his car, and his ability to purchase his supplies.

After six, two-hour sessions, it became very clear that two things were driving his business: the belief that price was the only thing, and his overwhelming need to be liked.

His desire to be liked stemmed from the continual rejection by his parents. His mother lived nearby and weekly reminded him of his inadequacies. His father never gave him the time of day.

It took a little while to get him to raise his prices, but because both his father and his mother rejected him at an early age, he would spend an inordinate amount of time socializing with each of his clients so that his productivity ended up being too low to effectively bring in the cash-flow he needed to make ends meet.

His necessity to be liked and accepted far outweighed his business logic.

**WTGB**—High quality can demand a higher price, if the market can bear it.

Currently, he is in weekly counseling sessions to help him deal with his poor self-image. Until he reconciles with this personal problem, we cannot help him grow his business.

Any one of the above scenarios, or a combination thereof, can contribute to your reluctance to bring your fees in step with the competition. Remember, if you are capturing more than 50% of the bid business and yet you are not making a profit but only have enough money to just make ends meet, you need a reality check. And, maybe not just of the price you are charging but of what drives your thought process.

For years, business analysts have operated with the belief that any business can be successful if the owner uses basic business practices within his organization. But the business owner has to be willing to change himself to accept the proper business practices.

I could tell you, and I'm sure you've heard it before, you have to surround yourself with competent people, and then delegate a part of your business operation to them, and let them do their jobs.

But, what I can't tell you is what is stowed away behind that third door on the left, inside your mind—the door that, as soon as you think of raising your prices, opens and something horrible reaches into your mind and squeezes until you choke from anxiety.

You'll never find a lock strong enough to keep that demon hidden away. He needs to be exposed and neutralized. Expose him and grow. Grow personally. Grow your business.

**WTGB**—Personal counseling may be the best investment you will ever make.

## Chapter 13

## Looking for Love in All the Wrong Places

One of the strongest human needs outside of the need for survival and self-preservation is the need to be loved, or liked. When this need is too strong in the need-bank of a business owner, he may make "heart-driven" decisions that may damage his company—perhaps even fatally. This need to be appreciated is sometimes so strong that it colors every facet of the entrepreneur's decision-making process.

This need to be loved, liked, appreciated is sometimes so strong, so dominant in an entrepreneur's psyche, he is unable to see clearly enough to make the correct business decisions.

A few years back, we had a client who owned a national company. He could not comprehend that if his men were busy and the company had payments coming in, he could be losing money. He operated all along the east and gulf coasts out of seven offices: Syracuse, Nashville, Dallas, Sarasota, Baltimore, Albany, and Boston.

Once the company was analyzed, and the pricing structure assessed, it became clear that the work was being quoted at a price much lower than what the company needed to net, let alone gross, from each job. As a result, the bid/award ratio was high. The men were always busy, the salesmen had great closing ratios, but the company was losing money.

Only one office was profitable: Baltimore. When the owner was presented with the flaw in his quoting procedure, his response was, "We'll lose jobs, and my men will sit home without work." He had two reasons to be worried about this.

His desire to be a hero to his men, creating a "we need him" dependency among his crew, was certainly providing work and an income for his squads but at the same time a loss for his company. We projected that within 15 months, he would be out of business.

Even after seeing the projections, and the impending loss scenario, he still would not price the jobs correctly. Finally, after showing him he would need to do 450 percent more work, manage a work force of more than 300 men (instead of the 16 he had), and perform 45 million square feet of new construction (working 24 hours a day) to net a one dollar year-end profit, he got the message.

But he suffered greatly. He suffered emotionally

because he knew his men would hate him because he would have to lay them off. (But remember I mentioned there was another reason.)

If he had kept going in the same direction, there would have been no work at all, ever again, for either him or his men.

In the end, he didn't have to lay the men off. We taught him how to properly price his service, and we set up procedures to increase sales by hiring a full-time estimator. Sales grew from under $1,000,000 to over $3,000,000 in two years, and he actually had to hire more men.

But the company was in bad shape. Over the years he had lost more than $300,000 in profits because of his need to be loved. He supplemented the loss of income by borrowing against his operating line that was now maxed out. He was looking for love in all the wrong places. His men would have really hated him if he had closed the company.

Just setting up proper pricing and educating him was not the solution to the problem. The solution was that he had to come to grips with what was driving his need to be liked by his men. We found out that he lived in a small rural town and he was the local hero for employing the people that lived day-to-day and hand-to-mouth in the hills surrounding the town.

He had never been the hero to anyone. In high school he was considered riffraff. Then one day, because of the efforts of his mother, taking it upon herself to create a resume and write a letter on his behalf, he was offered a job with a construction company operated by a gentleman with an engineering degree.

Eventually, he became a full partner in the company and was left to determine pricing and coordinate the workforce. It was the classic case of the tail wagging the dog. The men in the field, most never completing high school, were running the company—making demands, suggestions, calling the shots, and throwing temper tantrums if they didn't get their way. And because the hero wanted to be loved, liked, wanted, appreciated, he bent to their whims.

An analysis showed that the only reason the company existed was to keep the men in that small community employed, while the debt was growing and the company was heading toward bankruptcy.

You may wonder about the other partner. Couldn't he have put an end to this situation?

They were two peas in a pod, so to speak. Each of them had the same need. We never really found out the motivation of the other partner, but fortunately he stepped aside and allowed us to correct the situation and help the hero retain his champion status and yet operate the company profitably.

But remember I mentioned another reason the one owner was concerned he would have to lay his men off and lose their loyalty?

We were having trouble reconciling the payroll on all

the jobs against the hours worked and the projects completed. Then, one of our employees discovered that periodically, whole crews ended up missing in action.

This was explained away by the one owner as vacation time, etc. Because it was our responsibility to act as the interim general manager of the company, we began discreetly checking up on the foremen and the crews. We suspected that they were taking on work for other construction companies while they were employed by our client.

We had to resort to hiring a private investigator who, within thirty days, presented us with in-broad-daylight videotapes of foremen and crews working at sites that on paper in the home office didn't exist. According to the private eye, "the properties are owned by The Mob."

It was further uncovered that in order to finance a gambling problem, the small-town hero/owner contracted with a number of out-of-state companies and individuals that insisted on being paid only in cash.

He paid the crew with company funds and pocketed the revenue himself. He explained it as: "…the balance of payments on previous jobs that the company didn't have the money to pay when the jobs occurred." It seemed reasonable since many times they didn't have the money. But it was deceptive and illegal.

There is a lot more to this story. But let's just say, it read like a Mario Puzo novel. Our consulting-company employees began to fear leaving that client's office after dark and turning the keys in the ignitions of their cars.

About six years later and another client: This time the need to be needed manifested itself in the owner's continual compulsion to give a discount for his service. He called us in because he could not understand why, when all his people were busy, he barely had enough money to make ends meet. He and his employees had no benefits and no retirement. He had been operating his business for twenty years.

When we came in to do an analysis and uncovered no standardization in pricing, especially when the owner was involved, he quickly found a way to invite us on a leave of absence.

To this day we have not been paid—not because he is a corrupt or dishonest person, but because if he pays us, he would be admitting he was the main cause of his problems. And that would be too much for him to bear, especially since he has spent his entire business career blaming everyone else for his failures.

**WTGB**—Be careful who you blame for your problems. Remember the old "three fingers pointing back at you."

So what can someone do about this "I want to be needed" dilemma?

If you have this desire to be needed, do not become alarmed—everyone wants to be needed. Everyone wants to be loved, so wanting to be appreciated, even if you are the boss, is OK. The problem arises when your "need to be needed" overpowers your business logic. And on many occasions, if the striving for the satisfaction of these needs goes unchecked, it can have a major negative effect on your bottom line.

But what can you do to control these needs?

You must learn to look at the big picture. You need to ask yourself, "Where will I be in fifteen years operating as I am now? Will I have a profitable company that can give me a pleasant retirement, or will I have nothing, including a company that is worthless?" You need to be honest with yourself, because if you are not, you will be in a perpetual negative net-worth situation.

If, after you have asked these questions, and you find that you are going nowhere and you will have nothing at the end of fifteen years, then it is time you made some changes.

I am not referring to firing your staff. Your staff may be the reason you have lasted this long. And I am not saying fire yourself. What I am saying is maybe you need to have a closed-door session with yourself, and give yourself thirty days to get your act together.

You may need to set up some procedures that are hard, unbreakable rules within the company that even you must follow. Or maybe hire a consultant to help you.

Now, I know you think that this defeats the reason you went into business in the first place—to be independent and free of restraints—but more than anyone, you need to follow the rules, the rules of good business. If you don't, you'll be looking for appreciation in another place—someone else's business—but this time as an employee.

**WTGB**—Believe in yourself. You can do anything you set your mind to do.

## Chapter 14

## A Company Analysis—Part One

Ray Grishom drives a new pickup, lives in a $300,000 home that rests at the edge of a lake, sends his kids to private schools, goes on great vacations, eats out almost every weekend evening, and always picks up the tab when he is out with friends or relatives.

Ray is thirty-six years old. He came up the hard way. Growing up in a backwoods, North Carolina hilltop community, Ray barely had enough leather between his feet and the dirt roads he walked to school every day—to a school where the more fortunate kids made fun of him because he wore the same shirt day after day—not that he wanted to, but he only had two shirts.

One shirt was for school and one for church. He washed his school shirt every day, sometimes putting it on in the winter when it was still damp when the fire would go out and not warm his one room cabin where he lived with his aunt and uncle.

Ray's parents died when he was young. We don't know how; he won't talk about it.

This is not a scene from a novel written about a time long past. This is a true picture of a client in the Southwest.

Twenty-five years ago, Ray was living day to day. He grew up hating his situation and fighting the echoes of the kids at school who called him, "One-shirt-Ray." And along with many other insults about his financial situation, the kids insinuated that Ray was stupid. "One-shirt-Ray. Stupid, One-shirt-Ray."

Ray vowed he would never be one-shirted ever again. Nor let anyone know he was stupid, although deep down he thought he was. But his ego protected him.

And so, Ray worked hard, and kept one goal in mind (well two goals really: money and shirts). His closet was full of shirts—some were months old with the tags still on them. Every time he would go out with his wife to the mall, he would buy a shirt. He wore a Rolex on his wrist and walked like he owned the world. And each day, he wore a new shirt.

Ray ate the best food, and when he went away on vacation—three times a year for two weeks at a time—he would stay at the best resorts. The furniture in his home was special order, and his swimming pool was the envy of his friends and relatives.

Of course, it is interesting to note, and a common pattern amongst low-esteem people, that not one of Ray's friends was better off than Ray. In fact, most of his friends lived in low-income track homes, shacks or mobile homes.

Ray was the wealthiest man in his circle of friends.

A good test of someone's self-image is to look at the people with whom they surround themselves. If all their friends are less well off, less educated, and have less opportunity, then their self-image is not too strong. If, on the other hand, they have a balance of relationships—some better, some worse—usually their self-image is in equilibrium.

So, what does this have to do with running a business? Ray owns the business we are about to discuss. I give you his background so that you may understand how Ray got into his situation.

Walking into a new company, even under the protection of a signed contract, is always foreboding. From the boss right down to the employee who sweeps the floor, an attitude of suspicion permeates the atmosphere. They fear.

They fear the critical eye of the consultant. They fear his callousness, his objectivity, his detachment, his lack of understanding that, for the last 15 years, they have sold their souls to the company, and this consultant is going to come in and hack the company apart. Maybe even hack them. The hostility is masked with an over enthusiastic and cooperative attitude that soon fades.

The first question we asked: "Can I see your income-and-expense statement? Your profit-and-loss?" resulted in blank stares and was countered with, "Our accountant handles that."

Now, I hope you are not looking down your nose at this answer. There are many entrepreneurs out there operating somewhat profitable businesses who never see or understand a profit-and-loss statement. They entrust that job to their accountant. They have concentrated on what they do best and leave the financial aspects to those who are degreed in that discipline.

We recently worked with a client that when we walked in the door April $5^{th}$ and asked for the latest Profit and Loss figures, he informed us he had not seen anything from his accountant since November. He didn't even know how he had fared the previous year. Up to this point, he had run his business based on his gut feelings and by looking at his checkbook balance.

The only problem with this method of operation is that this business owner has, and Ray shares, an accountant who just crunches the numbers and makes no comments as to whether the company appears to be having financial problems. And although the account has been imputing information dutifully from the company check register and kicking out a monthly balance sheet and income statement, Ray has never looked at it. He figured he knew what he was making. There was money in the bank, he had the respect of his friends and relatives because he paid for their meals, and he wore a new shirt every day.

Ray was the boss, and everyone knew it. He arrived after everyone had reported to work, and he usually went out to lunch or had someone run and pick him up something. He paced the floor continually, never sitting down, always remaining visible.

His voice could be heard barking orders, yelling, reprimanding almost on the hour. He treated everyone like they knew nothing. He never wrote anything down—he prided himself on keeping everything in his head. He countermanded and second-guessed his employees continually.

So what did the analysis uncover? First off, there was no computerized bookkeeping program operating. Ray's wife, Laura, kept the books on a daily basis in a three-ringed binder. Deposits and checks were recorded as they occurred.

The right-hand drawer of the desk held the bills that were due. About every ten days or so, Ray would go through the drawer, look at the bills that were due, and decide which ones to pay and which to leave until the next time.

What measure did he use to make this decision? His gut. He made all decisions based on his instincts. The facts he used were what he knew at that moment in time—a snapshot of business savvy—a photo that faded quickly like a magic.

I feel I should tell you what type of business this is. It is actually three separate businesses.

Company A is a furniture sales and repair shop. There are fourteen assembly rooms, two paint booths, one of which cost $65,000 and is state-of-the-art. In one room stands rows and rows of paints with automated stirring wands rotating continuously. There are seventeen employees.

Company B buys and sells furniture at wholesale. This company has two employees. Furniture is bought at auctions and resold, as is, or refurbished by Company A and then sold.

Company C is a transportation company contracted by Company A or B to pickup and deliver the furniture. This company has one employee.

This year the consolidated sales of all three companies will exceed $5 million.

Ray has a number of habits that are going to be hard to break. Ray loves his cellular phone. He gives his number to everyone. Ray wants to feel indispensable. And he dials the phone whenever he gets a thought he needs to communicate or a question he needs answered. He also uses it to download data from myriad websites and fires off texts like his life depended on them.

Business lunches and dinners are his thing. He knows that the "wheelers and dealers" operate this way, and so does he. And of course, the company will pay for it, no matter how many there are at the table.

Ray wants to expand his business; he wants to buy the

building he is currently renting. When Ray began working in this particular industry, he was a partner in another person's business. The other person got into financial trouble.

Ray ended up on the short end of the stick, so he decided to go into business for himself to prevent that from happening again. His first business was the furniture store and repair business. He definitely knew how to fix furniture.

Soon however, Ray began to have problems securing enough business to keep his employees busy. So he started the furniture wholesale business so he could better control the potential for business for his first company.

Not too long after the creation of the second company, Ray became frustrated because he had to wait and be at the mercy of the transportation companies picking up and delivering his furniture. So, not being one to let anyone else control his situation, he created a transport company.

Are you seeing the pattern? Can you guess Ray's motivation?

Ray needs to be in control. He is insecure about the circumstances and untrusting of the people around him. Therefore, he has to take personal control of anything with which he is concerned.

If Ray's company had stayed small, he could have made a modest living; although his cash-flow would not allow him to live beyond day to day.

Unfortunately, he still is living from day to day—just on a bigger and more precarious scale. By the way, the business is in his wife's name because Ray declared bankruptcy a few years back.

Ray needs to accept his shortcomings and seek professional help to walk him through his forest of hang-ups. Until he does, he will always be in a financially precarious position and be in a continual state of anxiety.

**WTGB**—Understanding your weaknesses, strengthens you.

# Chapter 15

# A Company Analysis Part Two:

# Agony Before Ecstasy

In the last chapter, we talked about Ray and his furniture conglomerate. Well, it is time to help Ray with what he needs to do to turn his situation around. The following are the visible solutions. The root of his problem, his self-image, must also be addressed. But for now, let us explore the results of his self-image problem.

First of all, let us look at the list of the problems that needs to be addressed:
1) computerize accounting and bookkeeping
2) analyze the past 12 months
3) put a cash-management system in place
4) draw up a budget
5) do job-costing and expense-tracking
6) control spending; cut:
    a) excessive cellphone use
    b) meal expenses

    c)   entertainment costs
7) increase intra-company communication
8) reduce per-furniture acquisition price
9) increase per-furniture sales price
10) thoroughly investigate feasibility of acquiring building
11) address payroll concerns
12) draft a strategic sales plan
13) reduce debt to cut interest expense
14) review every aspect of supply purchasing—shop around—get the best price.
15) address shop efficiency
16) create an organizational chart to solidify reporting lines
17) prepare estimates for all work performed
18) track sales on a daily basis
19) track expenses on a daily basis
20) note whether businesses are cash or accrual—currently they are cash businesses (Going forward, we need to take a hard look at this.)
21) develop accounts payable and accounts receivable policies
22) develop employee incentive programs
23) create a logbook system that tracks what is happening every day
24) set up a chart of daily sales needed with a cumulative total and track daily sales for all companies
25) develop a business plan (Where is the company going?)
26) create timelines for each area of concern

If you remember, Ray's companies' combined sales exceeded $5 million. He must have been doing some things right. Right? Well, not really. He continued to borrow from his investors to pay bills and meet payroll.

His profits, such as they were, were used to cover his inadequate pricing, buying, and spending habits. Oh, one other thing, Ray was paying his people partly through a payroll service and also under the table. Although, he wasn't intentionally trying to cheat the government.

He paid his wife a huge salary for the work she did, paid the proper taxes and withholdings on the dollar amount, and then took some of her pay and divvied it up among his shop employees. We could not tell him we approved. We advised him to get out of the situation as soon as he could.

Of course, what drove this behavior was his need to be "The Man." And all his employees new that he was taking money out of his pocket and slipping it to them because he cared about them so much. He did care about his employees, but his methods were actually hurting them, and him.

We do not have the space to thoroughly discuss each of the above-listed items. And bear in mind, this is just a partial list of all the things needing attention. However, we will discuss a few on the list.

A cash-management system and policy, including a budget, is absolutely necessary if you intend to operate a profitable business—an "on purpose" profitable business. Many businesses operate profitably without a budget.

But the profits of a business are at the mercy of

everything in the world that could affect them—things like the world economy, the local economy, the health of the employees, the owner's health, the prices of supplies, the availability of supplies, the cost of transportation, postage, rent, insurance, taxes, employee attrition, natural disaster.

All these things, and more, affect your profits. And the best way to insure your company is profitable is to anticipate impacts on your eanings and put those thoughts down on paper in the form of a budget.

After the budget is in place, the most critical aspect of the money-management system is the discipline, or the "money management policy"—policies like no special, best-friend deals; no under-the-table payments; no emotional purchases. In other words, once the budget is in place, unless you seriously attempt to adhere to the line items in the budget, your budget effort will be for naught.

Ray admitted that one of the reasons he approached his investors to finance the purchase of his current business, was to have no rules placed on him by a bank. He hated structure. He wanted his options open at all times. So although he understood the need for a budget, he had a difficult time living within the constraints of one. He remembered having to live with only two shirts, and he vowed to never be in that situation again.

**WTGB**—Budgets free you—not bind you.

Another area that is critical in any business is the business plan. Ray knew where he wanted to go. Eventually he wanted to own the block, the street, maybe even the town someday. He wanted to make money and employ more people. He wanted to grow his business into a mega-conglomerate empire.

The only problem with Ray's plan was his attention to detail. He gave no thought or time to writing down how he was going to achieve his goals or how he was going to finance his growth. Remember, he prided himself on keeping everything in his head.

**WTGB**—Keep your mind free for creative thinking and problem solving. Do not use your mental energy trying to remember things that could be written down on a piece of paper and reviewed daily.

Unless Ray commits to paper his goals and a plan to reach those goals, he will never uncover the problems and challenges to reach those goals. And, consequently, he will probably never reach them.

**WTGB**—Buy a spiral notebook to record your short-term goals.

Place today's date in the left column of the first page and jot down bullets of things you need to accomplish. When the next day arrives, jot down that date and the things that come to mind that day. When you accomplish one of the tasks, place a check mark next to it. If you determine you did not have to do a task, cross it out with a single thin line. Or use whatever method of tracking that suits you.

Carry the notebook everywhere you go—within reason of course. Look at it before you leave the house, before you leave work, before you leave your car, after you get to work, after you get into your car. Each time you move, look at it.

Another critical area is the strategic sales plan. Once you have determined the budget and set in motion the hard-and-fast rules of money management, the income needs to be generated to cover the expense items in your budget. This income is a result of your sales effort and the cost of sales.

## But what is the strategic sales plan, and what does it entail?

1. Determine the sales/marketing area to be covered by the company. This should be done based on the available resources to aid in the sales process—i.e., brochures, letters, mailers, telemarketing, sales staff, ability to follow-up. Once the geographic area is determined, then the best sales methods must be decided—i.e., mailers and follow-up phone calls, sales calls and follow-up letters; telemarketing and follow-up sales calls; Web page, etc.

2. Determine your ideal target customers. What do they do? Where do they do it? How do they do it? If your potential customer is a business, what is its size? Create a customer profile. This is determined by the kind of customer with which you wish to be working, not necessarily the customer base with which you are already exploiting. However, you should know what kind of customer you attract, and build a profile of that customer, too.

3. Determine who would be implementing the sales effort—who would be making sales. Then determine the amount of time available to be devoted to sales.

4. Schedule the sales effort. This is probably the most critical portion of the sales process. Many companies fail because although they have great sales strategies, no one implements them. Schedule your entire week on paper—not in your head.

5. Analyze the results of your sales efforts and make the necessary adjustments to reach your goals.

**WTGB**—Looking back over what you have done can help you plan what you should be doing in the future.

We now need to discuss the organizational structure of Ray's company—not whether it is a corporation or a DBA, but who is in charge? Who makes the decisions? To whom does the office staff report? To whom do the shop employees report?

After observing the daily operations of Ray's company, it became very clear that the employees reported to whoever gave them the best deal at that particular time.

For instance: at 2:30 PM, Ray would go out into the shop and instruct one of his employees to fix a particular piece of furniture by 5:00 PM. Within fifteen minutes, Ed, Ray's right-hand man, would walk out into the shop and see that a job that had to be done by 4:00 PM, which he had assigned to that same repairman, was abandoned and replaced by a piece Ed had never seen before.

The shop worker knew that if he did what Ray told him to do; he would receive a few extra dollars under the table. What he did not know was that the item Ed wanted finished was going to make substantially more money for the company than the rush-job Ray assigned. Ray needs to settle on one person, preferably Ed, to whom the shop employees report. And Ray needs to filter all his personal jobs through Ed.

But can Ray really relinquish that authority and still feel in control? Currently, no. He actually has to be in control at all times. When he is away on vacation, he calls a couple of times a day, even though he has a more-than-capable second-in-command who has better people-skills and fewer skeletons in his closet than Ray.

The last item we will have room to discuss is Ray's ego, or rather his poor self-image. And the only thing we can say is Ray needs to go to counseling to get rid of those school kids in his brain who keep taunting him to spend his and the company's money so freely. Ray needs to control that side of his memory so he can be free to operate his business professionally and more profitably.

We are giving Ray time to catch up to the computer world, but in the meantime, he has reverted back to spending freely and always picking up the tab at dinner. He held the urge in check for a while with the help of his wife, but Ray's old habits are going to be hard to break, especially because the voices in his brain are so loud.

**WTGB**—Give yourself a periodic reality check. Do not second-guess your decisions, but try to understand why you made them.

# Chapter 16

## An Exercise:

## The Cause or the Symptoms

A while ago, I spent some time with a friend who owns six businesses in Denver. We were having a casual conversation over a couple of drinks when he asked why, after all these years our company had not hooked up with the larger consulting firms. He then proceeded to reap accolades on a national consulting company he had read a lot about. I told him that ten years ago we were offered an opportunity to coop with that very company, but turned it down when we discovered how they operated.

Now, I am not generalizing and lumping all consulting companies into one large ineffective category, but I did know the track record of this one company and, although it charged an exorbitant rate and had financially-degreed employees by the hundreds, the company only really provided its clients with bandages and salve, but no cure.

Why? Because this company addressed the results of the problem—the symptoms—not the cause. They set up extravagant accounting procedures that if followed, would help stabilize any business. But they didn't address the reason these procedures were not installed in the first place.

The cause of any business problem without exception (not withstanding circumstances beyond human control) can always can be traced back to a human being, a person—manager, owner, president—and either a personality flaw or an educational short-coming.

**WTGB**—If there are areas within your company you are unfamiliar, either learn them or hire someone who knows them.

So, how can a small business person—an entrepreneur—guarantee he makes the correct business decisions to move his business forward?

It is understandable that the skin of an entrepreneur must be thick. She must be willing to undergo great scrutiny by the financial industry and detached suspicion by her business associates. The downside of this thick skin is that it sometimes causes the entrepreneur to turn her back on good advice or to continually second-guess advice.

An example of this: You have turned a function over to a subordinate and then, because you get impatient, end up taking it back and doing it yourself.

**WTGB**—If after you have turned a project over to an employee and you suspect it is falling behind, there is nothing wrong with helping the employee. Just don't take it away from the employee.

**WTGB**—Only by allowing the employee to struggle, will the employee grow in value.

An interesting experience occurred while involved with a local chapter of the Jaycees. The current president, who had aspirations of one day running for Congress, was a micromanager. He would continually be on the phone harassing the other volunteers and stepping in to say, "I'll take care of that."

One of the purposes of the Jaycees was to breed strong community and business leaders, giving them the opportunity to experience real responsibility. The only problem with this local organization was that it bred weak business leaders because the president always stepped in to bail out the novices—never allowing growth.

When a business owner continually steps in to take over a project, make a phone call, or finish a report, he is enabling incompetent subordinates. Actually, what happens is they begin to do a less-than-complete job, knowing that the boss is going to redo it anyway.

Think about it. What if after you cleaned your room, your mother came in and re-cleaned it? You might as well have watched TV.

And so many kids do. And this same approach carries on into business if the boss does the same sort of thing.

If you are a small-business owner, here is a simple exercise you should perform once every six months. Ask yourself these questions:

1) Do you know everything there is to know about operating a business?

2) Can you perform every function within your business in the most efficient manner?

3) Do you stay abreast of changing laws that affect your business?

4) Do you have a degree in human-resource management, business administration, finance, marketing, advertising, design, sales management, training, computer technology—and on and on?

5) Do you think asking for help is a sign of weakness?

6) Do you think you can learn from your competition?

7) Do you think you can learn from your customers?

8) Do you think you can learn from your friends?

9) Do you think you can learn from your employees?

10) Do you think you can learn from your spouse?

This list is by no means complete, but if you begin

with these questions, then others will form in your head and you will be forced to undergo a self-analysis.

But how should you answer these questions? The first question should be answered with a NO. If you answered YES, then you are above any other business owner in the world. But if you answered NO, then you need to explore those areas within which you lack knowledge and set about to have someone teach you or hire someone to help you get a handle on those sections of your business.

**WTGB**—Surrounding yourself with employees who are smarter than you, never brought a business into ruin.

Question number 5 is a real psychoanalytical teaser. If you ask for help, aren't you showing that there is an area you do not understand? Won't this clearly state, "I don't know," and show you are weak?

Actually, what it really says is, "I realize I cannot know everything, I am only one person. So, therefore, I must find experts in the areas within which I lack knowledge and ask them to help me grow my business."

That seems to be a statement of confidence and strength rather than weakness. You have to forget those kids in school who made fun of you when you said you did not know the answer or raised your hand to ask the teacher for help. Those kids are not in your life now, and if anyone around you makes fun of your honesty and integrity in admitting you do not know something and need help, I suggest you question their motivation and friendship.

What if you identified several areas where you admitted to yourself you were weak in knowledge and experience? The best thing you could do is swallow your pride and seek out individuals who are the best in those given disciplines to help you with your company.

What would happen to your business if you had the best people available working there? What if every so often you had a meeting with these experts? How healthy would your business be if you did this?

**WTGB**—Create an advisory board for your company.

This board may be the only way you can maintain any business balance. It will keep you going in the right direction. It will help smooth out your rough edges and the potentially negative financial impact on your business.

Number 9 can be an eye-opener. One of the first things we do when we take on a new client is set up a schedule to interview each employee. After the interviews, we have a pretty fair understanding of all the areas that need attention. We even have a hint as to why the company needs help, and what quirk within the owners psyche is causing the most trouble.

We usually do not learn what the root of the problem is, but sometimes we do. Sometimes one of the employees knows that when the owner was seventeen, she was raped by her stepfather and holds her mother responsible. That is why she treats the older women in the company with such contempt, never listening to their ideas.

Many times your employees have a better understanding of what is needed to help the company than anyone else. Collectively, they are a great board of directors.

The only other question to which I wish to draw your attention is question #10. Your spouse may have more insight into what might be right with your business, as well as what might be wrong. And specifically, right and wrong with you. Having a monthly board meeting with your spouse may move you forward more quickly than a meeting with any other business associate. And don't get caught up in old Neanderthal thoughts like, "She doesn't understand my business."

She understands you. She understands people, and she may have a better, more objective perspective of your employees than you. And living with you day-in and day-out and getting to know your parents and some of your friends, she may have a pretty solid grasp as to why you have become the person you are. So have a monthly meeting. Start out at a restaurant. Who says board meetings can't be fun?

By the way, the national company at the beginning of this chapter that my friend praised, is no longer in business, forcing to close its operations after suffering legal suits for its criminal handling of another major national company.

# Chapter 17

# Conclusion

This book has been written for one purpose and one purpose only: to bring to light the fact that many of the problems that small-business owners encounter in their attempt at running a company are sometimes self-imposed or as a result of inadequacies within themselves. And these failings could be the result of emotional glitches in their psychological make-up.

I have not tried to explain away business problems by saying most small companies are run by a bunch of misfits. Nor have I tried to solve the problems that manifest themselves in poor cash flow, sinking sales, and low profits.

All I have attempted to do is to alert those business owners that have a real desire to improve their bottom line to the idea that they themselves may be holding back the company.

In fact, during our interviews with the staff of most companies, the employees actually state that the company would operate a lot more efficiently if the owner would stay on vacation. And in looking at the financial record of the companies that have come to us for help, we can see a more business-like approach exercised by the staff when the boss is gone than when she is in her office.

I am not saying that all of a company's problems can be traced back to the owner, but many can.

We were contracted by a physician to get his computer software company off the ground. When we arrived on site, the employees could not wait to tell us that the doctor had been trying to start the company for two years. He had hired a long line of people with varied backgrounds and soon dismissed them one by one claiming they were incompetent. In fact, according to him (so the employees said) everyone was incompetent.

We got the message loud and clear. We knew we were going to be ineffective—he would prove us incompetent, too. And he did.

We struggled for ten months. But the doctor was a micromanager. He did not trust anyone else's judgment and continually second-guessed his staff and us. He was manic.

To all of his staff, he would frequently send email messages at 3:00 in the morning and then call them at 8:30 AM for the answers to his questions. One employee had fourteen separate emails from the owner sent between 11:00 PM and 5:30 AM.

He called at 8:30 AM and asked for the answers. If his employees lived in France today, as a result of a new law that went into affect January 1, 2017, they wouldn't be obligated to read or respond to his emails after hours and before the workday began. But in the US, it is expected that workers stay connected even when they are home or on vacation.

In the operating room he could not make a mistake. He had assistants with him, but he was the person operating and the one responsible. He had complete control. He loved it. But outside the operating room, he didn't have absolute control, so he forced himself on everything and everyone.

Tired of his abuse, we fired ourselves from the situation.

It has now been five years and his computer software company is still not operating—and he still keeps going through employees and consultants, claiming they are incompetent.

**WTGB**—Very rarely is an employee incompetent. Usually only 1 out of 100 is incompetent, and that may be as a result of being placed in the wrong job based on the employee's skills and education. A square peg in a round hole if you will.

We just finished with a client who made all the company's financial decisions based on the Blue-Light Specials being run at the time. I am not attempting to poke fun at a very successful company and its use of an innovative marketing tool. I wish to hit square in the eyes, those business owners who seem to always make decisions on price alone and always look for the least expensive way out of a problem rather than looking for the proper solution no matter the cost.

These same people dine at the finest restaurants, wear the best clothes, and travel to the most expensive resorts; but they Band-Aid their company's equipment together, give minuscule raises, and stall forever when it comes to making any innovative moves that would mean money leaving the company and not going into their own pockets.

Why is this?

Why would a business owner not want to invest quality back into his or her own business?

**WTGB**—Assess your long-range goals. Is it to work in your company until you die, or is it to work in your company in the hopes of retiring one day? If you have to use the sale of your company as a retirement fund, you cannot be spending it on yourself ahead of time.

If you really wish to be successful enough to retire on a good pension or sell your business for a good price, you must reinvest quality back into your company. And I don't mean using Blue-Light Specials.

I feel sorry for business brokers. I have had occasion to work with a number of them, and I could not tell you how many times they would send me a prospectus on a business and the asking price of the owner, and after I did the business valuation, I would find that it was only worth a fraction of what the owner was asking or believed it was worth. So what happened to these businesses?

Many times the owner looses interest in managing the company, begins to take long weekends, begins to come in late and leave early, and turns his back on the growing number of equipment breakdowns. He has worked in the company for seventeen years and is ready to get out of the responsibility.

He has eaten the best food, bought the most expensive clothes, lives in a house in an exclusive area that has more than enough space, drives a new car, is seen at the big society functions, and wears a great tan.

Now he wants to retire and continue living that same great lifestyle and so has placed a value on his company that exceeds its worth by one hundred times.

The money that should have gone back into the company was spent on an extravagant lifestyle. Now the company is basically worthless.

That is why I feel sorry for business brokers, because they have to listen to these business owners tell them how valuable their business is, put it on the market, and find no one interested because the company is not worth the asking price.

So what causes this discrepancy in the actual business value and the asking price of the owner?

**Greed.**

And that is exactly what was at play with the client I mentioned earlier. He wanted to sell his company so he asked if we would come in and make it profitable. He had already spent his retirement, but he affixed a $525,000 price tag on a business that had a going concern value of a negative -$15,000.

In order for us to successfully turn the company around, we had to remove the owner from the daily operations of the company. Once we did that, profits began to increase and equipment, long since neglected, became efficient again.

We had another occasion where an owner asked us to turn his company around so he could sell it. We could not get it to where he wanted it because he continually fought our advice. He ended up selling it for a substantial loss. He could not bring himself to let go so we could help. He paid us, but he could not let go. A year later he admitted it, but of course it was too late.

**WTGB**—Do not be afraid to let go.

All the examples I have cited are real. They all could have been corrected with one simple solution: the owner of the business needed to learn more about himself to uncover his unique quirks, deal with them, and learn how to apply a new approach to his business.

We have recommended personal counseling about 75% of the time. The rest of the time, we were able to put controls in place in the hands of strong employees who could keep the boss in check.

And so what can you do to help yourself? Hire an honest person who is not afraid to tell you the truth.

We have had our contracts abruptly terminated because the owner of a business did not appreciate our solutions to his business problems. We have lost money for sure, but not credibility.

But other than hiring someone what can you do?

Create a board of directors. It does not have to be a big board—just a few business-savvy people who will give you their honest opinions of your business direction. You can have meetings across a kitchen table or in the park if you like. The main thing is to have these meetings to discuss your problems, concerns, goals, dreams.

Now, I would like to say a short word about including your spouse in your business. I can only tell you of our experiences. As soon as the spouse becomes involved in the planning, problem-solving, and brainstorming of the small business, the business begins to stabilize and improve. This has happened without exception.

We do not know yet why this is, but we're trying to understand it so we can communicate it. Maybe it has something to do with "opposites attract." So, actually, your shortcomings are covered by the strengths of your spouse.

For the first time, as a test, we asked one of our new clients to include his wife (she stays home and takes care of their children) to attend our planning and problem-solving meetings with our client. Up until her participation, progress had been slow—it was like pulling teeth to get the owner to cooperate. As soon as his wife entered the picture, he became a dream to work with, and the company is turning around faster than we had anticipated.

Now, regarding the ego:

Unfortunately, because of the nature of the ego within someone who could be the problem, if the ego is uncontrolled, the business owner usually is unwilling to listen to anyone. So we are stuck. Remember at the very beginning, I asked if you had the emotional and psychological make-up to operate a business? Well, now it is time to revisit that question.

Can you handle being named as part of your company's problems? Can you admit you have some shortcomings? Can you bring yourself to a point to do the right things to grow—to increase your knowledge in an area within which you lack expertise? To hire someone who knows more than you? To seek counseling to help you unleash those gremlins in your head and free you up to make unprejudiced business decisions?

You had the entrepreneurial guts to start a business, or maybe you are just thinking about it. Do you have the backbone to make yourself a better boss, leader, or person?

"Ay, there's the rub." *Hamlet's soliloquy*-Shakespeare

It takes guts to admit that there could be something wrong with you. It takes strength of character. It takes a real entrepreneur.

If you really want to succeed, get rid of all the obstacles. Start from within, and the outside will follow.

Want to be a profitable business owner? Understand your # 1 employee!

You.

Grow you—grow your profits.

# ABOUT THE AUTHOR

Richard F. Corrigan graduated from the Maxwell School of Citizenship and Public Affairs at Syracuse University and resides with his wife Diana in Sarasota, Florida.

Positions held:
1. Youth Worker for a Chicago-based Interfaith Organization
2. Internal Auditor/Troubleshooter for a NYS Bank
3. Sales Manager of a national insurance company
4. Asst. Vice President of a commercial leasing company
5. Vice President of a NYS bank holding Company
6. President of a small business consulting company
7. Chief Operating Officer of a property management company
8. Nonprofit Organization Consultant and Board Facilitator
9. Middle School and High School Teacher

He has published various short stories, including: "They Heard the Music Together" in *RiverSedge*; "Suspended Life" in *The Pepper Tree;* "We Only Confess it to Ourselves" in *Writers Of The Desert Sage*; "Escaping the Congo" in *Whistling Fire*; "Jasmine, Wilting in the Garden" in *Red Fez;* "Vincent" in *Meat for Tea*; "Old Abigail Worthy" in *Clare Literary Journal;* and "Oscar de Paris" in *The MacGuffin*.

More information at http://www.richardfcorrigan.com/ www.facebook.com/RFCorrigan

November 2013, signed a multi-book (series) publishing contract with Zharmae Publishing. KRYSTAL VIBRATION SERIES (KRYSTAL VISION) published April 28, 2016 available at Amazon.com.

Email: 1krystalvision@gmail.com

www.ingramcontent.com/pod-product-compliance
Lightning Source LLC
Chambersburg PA
CBHW071439180526
45170CB00001B/384